Sara—
Thank you for your
support! I hope the
book inspires you and
you enjoy it!
Keep Moving Forward!
Adrienne Kallweit

Experiencing Love

An inspirational journey of fear turned faith, of
tumult turned harmony, of death turned life.

ADRIENNE ELAINE KALLWEIT

Two Thousand Nine Publishing

Illustrations, cover photos and graphics by Brooke Allen, Ballen Photography and Design. Interior photos used by permission from family members.

Printed in the United States of America.

ISBN-13: 978-1463581305
ISBN-10: 1463581300

This book is dedicated to my family:
David, Canaan, Ethan and Bella.

In this space and time we have here on Earth,
I am so thankful to spend it with you.

"Mom, why did God put us here on Earth? We are born. We play all the time. And then we die."

"I don't know the exact answer Canaan, but I do know that while on Earth, God wants us to **Experience Love**."

May, 2008
Conversation with Canaan, 8 years old

CONTENTS

I won't let my fears stop me, I am determined and have strength to move forward in all that I do.

In 2009 our family went through a life-threatening experience that rocked our world. Miraculously, through it all I had strength every step of the way. People often said to me during this experience, "I don't know how you are so strong," or "I don't know how you are doing it." And before you know the story of how I did it, how I stayed strong, how I didn't fear, you must first know that I was born a very fearful person.

I had typical childhood fears. From the time I was very young I was afraid of most everything. (Likely very annoying to my family when taking me anywhere.) I remember having to sit in the manager's office at a Ripley's Believe It or Not Museum on a family vacation because the wax figures scared me so much I wouldn't even walk past the Marilyn Monroe in the lobby. I even spent an entire day at a waterpark on the lifeguard's stand during another family vacation because I was afraid of the water rides *and basically everything at the park.* But my fearful nature continued into adulthood and became more focused on the big three: Tornados, Flying and Water!

Tornados. I am deathly afraid of thunderstorms and mostly the ones that can possibly at any instant produce a tornado. Growing up in Oklahoma the news coverage on a storm that may contain tornados is like slow motion coverage of a car wreck: Following its deadly trek through each town, tracking the time it will hit our home, warning us to take cover and then reporting of the death toll and destruction as the tornado passes into another susceptible area. The question is how could you not be fearful of tornados in Oklahoma after watching the news and as a result - tornado storm shelters are a great business to go into in Oklahoma!

Whenever a thunderstorm rolls through town I take caution and if there is even mention of a tornado I run to take cover. I have been known to pull a full size mattress into a bathroom or closet to hide underneath its fortress on numerous occasions and even into adulthood – at 5'5", 120 pounds and very limited muscle mass, adrenalin powers every mattress launching!

My oldest memory of the tornado fear is on one Easter Sunday when I was about six. A thunderstorm was approaching our neighborhood and the weatherman announced that our neighborhood was under a tornado warning. I remember running all by myself to the bathtub to huddle up under blankets and pillows as my entire family watched the beauty of the storm roll into town from our back deck. While hiding under a blanket and all the pillows I could pull off my bed, I realized I had left my favorite Easter basket on the back porch. I immediately imagined it being sucked up like Dorothy into the evil funnel, leaving Toto behind. I ran out of the bathroom and found my family had returned inside as the rain and hail had begun. I turned to my dad and begged him to go out and grab my Easter basket. But instead of helping he said, "Adrienne, if you want your basket you have to go out and get it!" I remember being so mad at him for not getting my special Easter basket for me but even at that young age I knew he was trying to teach me a lesson.

I stood at the window for what seemed to be hours contemplating if I was brave enough to go out in the deadly torrent. There came a lull in the storm and the thunder seemed to have slowed and I thought this must be the perfect opportunity to make my break to rescue my basket. I ran out to the porch and grabbed the basket and at that moment the lightning struck. Lightning and then thunder so loud that no one could hear my screams over the cacophony of the electric storm, and I made it back into the house, soaking wet, but with my basket and its treasured Easter eggs intact.

My dad was proud of me for being brave. He gave me a hug and said proudly, "See, you are OK, aren't you?" Through tears and still shaking with terror, I replied, "No!" I obviously didn't appreciate the lesson.

As an adult I knew I had to manage this fear so we built a Safe Room in our house, a concrete box attached to the slab of our house. Now I love the beauty of storms. That is, as long as I am home and within an arm's reach of the Safe Room.

Flying. I share this fear with my mom and although she may have passed some of this anxiety onto me, this is again another fear overly exaggerated by watching too much TV. The media's coverage of plane crashes would send anyone into a brief anxiety attack, but the thing about those little "horror news stories" is that the memory of the harrowing escapes from the plane crashes is stored in the susceptible person's memory bank, ready to recall while boarding every flight.

My first job out of college put me on the road for

eight months. I would have to spend two days of each week in the air and even now in our business I spend over 20 days a year in the air. I never let my fear of flying stop me from moving forward in life and doing the things I need to do but the fear will always be a part of me. I have read books, tried relaxation methods, and I am very logical and completely understand the fact that flying is much safer than traveling by car. But no matter how much I have studied about aerodynamics and jet engines and how flight is possible, every time I'm in a plane I just think we people inside the contraption are victims who are going to fall out of the sky and perish down below. So I reluctantly sit through every flight trembling with anxiety from every bump, whoosh and clang of the plane restlessly awaiting the pilot's announcement that we have (safely) made it to our destination.

Boats, lakes, oceans – basically anything that is near or related to water. I'm not sure why the fear of drowning has been such a deep seated fear of mine but ever since I was young I have been afraid of deep water. I have always been a great swimmer and we even had a pool in our backyard growing up; however, I never ventured to the deep end fearing that I would immediately get sucked down into the dark abyss of the drain at the bottom of the pool. (That is where Jaws lives, you know!) I was ten years old and on a boat ride with my family in the middle of a big deep lake and a thunderstorm rolled in. The thunderstorm alone scared me but to add insult to injury, my very ornery older brother began to taunt me about the boat sinking in the middle of the lake. My parents' attention was occupied with getting us safely back to shore and navigating the boat, not mediating the taunting I was receiving in the middle of the tumultuous lake.

We made it back safely that day and ironically we spent every summer at that same lake going out in our family boat. But for many years following that horrific lake experience with my brother, I would either refuse to go in the boat, or if I did I would tremble with fear as I lay on the floor of the vessel ...holding on for dear life.

When I entered college I realized this fear was getting a little ridiculous and decided that I had to conquer my anxiety of deep water. I decided the best solution would be to become a lifeguard so I could not only save other people's lives, but mine as well.

So basically I am not much fun to sit next to on a flight traveling across a body of water during a spring storm.

As you can see, I've spent most of my life challenging myself to face my innate fears, finding a way to conquer them so that I can get on with life. I work hard to never let my fears stop me from moving forward.

As I got older I began to evaluate my fearful nature and why it is that I am afraid of everything. Surely my brother's taunting me when I was younger wasn't the root of all my fears. From deeper evaluation, I would come to realize that almost all my fears revolved around one fear, the biggest fear - death.

In 2009 I conquered that fear and this is the story.

CHAPTER ONE

LEARNING
TO PRAY

Take some time to get to know God and He will teach you how to pray.

Is this really happening? Thoughts of anger began to race through my mind as the ER doctor was describing David's prognosis. Anger, because I just knew they had no clue what they were talking about, they must have gotten it wrong. "Are you sure?" Unable even to look me in the eyes the doctor replied, "Yes Ma'am." I paused then asked, "What should I do?" He answered, "You should call family," and then he walked down the hallway of St. John ER leaving me standing there, alone outside of David's room.

As soon as he walked away the anger changed to a rush of complete fear, fear that I was about to lose my husband and best friend. Is this really happening? We were just laughing together this morning, how can life change so quickly? In a state of shock, I walked outside of the ER to call family and as I walked I began to pray for David, the one

thing I absolutely knew I could do to help. And to think that, although a devoted Christian since birth, I didn't even know how to pray until just a few years earlier.

As a young mother, having a fellow-mom friend is vital for sanity. That is what Brecka was for me during those first years of motherhood and thank goodness she lived right across the street! Between the time David and I went from a family of three to a family of five, Brecka was my morning coffee, a safe place, a good laugh. We would spend time together unloading about the trials of motherhood while laughing in each other's chaos. With our growing family, David and I were starting a new business and building a new house; our every waking moment was on overload. Brecka's friendship was the greatest outlet I could have ever been blessed with during one of the most stressful times of my life.

I met Brecka at Jenks middle school and we lived a mile apart in Tulsa, Oklahoma. We would ride our bikes to each other's houses. That was back in the day when it was "safe" at eleven years old to holler to mom in the kitchen, "I am going to Brecka's," and get an "OK, be back by dinner." Later, we attended the same college and shared similar friends over the years. Even following college when Brecka moved out of the area, we had always managed to keep in touch.

After Brecka married she and her husband decided to move back to their hometown region of Tulsa where they built a new house in the country area of Catoosa. As a life-long Tulsan, I was unaware that we even had a town nearby Tulsa called Catoosa. I faintly remembered Catoosa as one of the cattle towns depicted in the musical *Oklahoma*. Growing up in Tulsa, which is about as cultured as any other large metropolitan U.S. city, Catoosa sounded like some serious Oklahoma country livin'. So my only reaction when she called to tell me they were moving to Catoosa was, "Where's Catoosa?"

Nevertheless, after Brecka's return to Oklahoma we lost touch for about eight months until David and I were on a lazy Sunday drive attempting to calm our colicky crying first-born and passed a highway marker for Catoosa.

I excitedly grabbed my cell phone and called Brecka. She is the kind of comfortable person that no matter how much time has gone by since our last conversation we can always pick up right where we left off. Brecka answered the phone on the first ring and without the usual salutation I asked, "Don't you live in Catoosa now?" I could hear Brecka's smile bouncing off the cell phone tower and into my ear, "Well, yes we do! Are you coming to visit me?" I told her I thought we were close to her and she gave me directions to her house – and Wow! What we found was beyond what we could ever expect to find in an obscure little town like Catoosa.

That short twenty minutes from the center of downtown Tulsa led us to a jewel of hills, rocks, trees and creeks. Their beautiful custom-built house was tucked away in a vibrant neighborhood of grand and charming homes. The visit was warm and welcoming. We commented on how beautiful it was out in Catoosa and before the day was over we found ourselves looking at lots in the neighborhood. We had no intentions of moving from where we were currently living, but ended up listing our house for sale and starting construction in Catoosa a month after our visit with Brecka.

With degrees in Construction Management for both David and myself, building a house was an undertaking that we had always wanted to do and knew we had the resources to accomplish. We took on the adventure with our firstborn in tow and his brother growing in my tummy. At the time we were moving to Catoosa and starting construction, I was

two years into an entrepreneurial journey that David and I had chosen for its flexibility for our my family. This *flexibility* allowed for mommy time, managing my home business and acting as construction manager on our "dream house." Quickly the tasks on my plate turned to chaos and Brecka's friendship was a happy distraction.

Brecka's best friend was her younger sister Amber and they both worked for the same employer, a bank in Tulsa. Both tall, blonde with inviting blue eyes that always smiled, the sisters were as close as two siblings could get without being twins. Brecka and Amber talked on the phone or in person at least ten times a day and when they weren't talking they were emailing or texting each other. They spoke the same language and when you were with them they always made you feel loved and joyful. They never made me, as an outsider, feel that I was intruding upon their friendship – on the contrary, they always invited me into their world.

Amber's visits were always welcome when Brecka and I as next-door neighbors would get together for morning coffee or evening cocktails. One of my favorite memories of my life is Brecka, Amber and I simply enjoying the day or watching the setting sun while the kiddos played under our feet.

Then everything right and beautiful about our life in Catoosa was annihilated by one evil act of violence. Amber was killed that year, 2004, by an armed bank robber.

Brecka lost part of herself with Amber's death and everything around Brecka's life changed. I could never know the depth of sorrow that Brecka experienced with the horrific loss of her sister, but my grief was a gnawing pain that wouldn't go away. I didn't know how to deal with it since I knew it wasn't appropriate to go to Brecka for support – I felt like my sadness paled in comparison to what she was going through. I talked with David about Amber's violent death and the void that her passing had left in

Brecka's and my relationship, and he realized that I was not only mourning Amber's death but also the loss of Brecka's friendship. Like Brecka losing Amber, I had lost my friend, my laughing place. I too was a casualty of the shooting.

Almost immediately following Amber's death I was no longer an integral part of Brecka's life and although before we were not best friends, we had a place for each other in a special time of our life. Her life moved on as she gravitated to people who had been employees at the bank at the time of Amber's murder, and to a close-knit group of other friends and family. The sudden loss of Brecka's friendship that came unexpectedly and without warning devastated me but I understood Brecka's actions and respected the changes in her life as she and her family were doing all they could to heal. I stepped away and we grew apart.

The stresses of that catastrophic event and the stresses of my own life had begun to take a toll on my mental well-being. In my head I was all over the place, in confusion, in depression, not to mention during that time I found out I was pregnant with our third child. My emotions were going completely out of whack fast. I spent the next few weeks constantly crying and took the stress out on my husband, the one who supported and loved me the most.

As the kids napped one afternoon, I took a walk outside to calm my nerves and check the mail. It was a steaming August afternoon and the heat on our asphalt driveway burned my feet but I didn't care – *If only something or someone could help deliver me from the awful burning emotions inside*, was the only thought I had as I put my hands up in the air and pleaded to God for help. As a Presbyterian, I fall into the nicknamed group "The Frozen Chosen" due to feeling very awkward with any kind of charismatic worship, so the raised hands were a very uncomfortable experience but I had nowhere else to turn – but up. I looked up and called, *God, Please help me. Please*

21

deliver me from this stress. Please show me why this happened to Amber. Why am I so unhappy when I have so much? Why did I lose my friend Brecka?

After I made my plea to God, I put my hands down and finished my journey to the mailbox. Inside was only one piece of mail. An 8 ½ x 11 piece of hot pink paper folded in half with the return address from our church. I opened the flyer that was addressed to me, literally and spiritually, and it read:

Moms on Mondays

Are you a mom that needs a break?
Are you struggling with the stresses of motherhood?
Do you feel lost in your day?

Join our mom's group, gain support from other moms and come closer to God

❖

FREE Childcare provided

I couldn't believe it; my prayer to God seemed to have been directly answered. I was so relieved that I began to cry right there in the driveway and called out, "Thank you, God." Then smiled with the thought, *What an ingenious way to spread the word of God, enticement through free childcare!*

Of course when you get a sign like that you answer it, right? I was desperate, what did I have to lose?

The Moms on Monday Bible study group was led by a wonderful mentor, a doctor's wife, Joli. She revealed a lot of her inner self to our class, some of which was surprising to me. Joli seemed to feel as if she was not worthy of teaching our class the virtues of being a better mom, wife and follower of Christ because it seemed to her that she was not always handling her personal trials and tribulations in a Christ-like manner. Like she said once, "I am a sinner teaching you." I wish I could have told Joli that her humble vulnerability is what made the lessons we studied so impactful. It was that she was *real*, like us; and as for me, knowing that Joli struggled every day to be worthy of God's love, it empowered me to work hard to be a worthy disciple of Christ.

Joli brought the Bible Study format with her to Tulsa from Alabama where her husband was completing his two-year medical residency. Because the course so profoundly changed her relationship with God, she felt a compelling calling to bring those lessons back to Oklahoma to share what she had learned with other moms. With me.

Even though the course came at a difficult time of my life, I didn't go into it with great expectations for the lessons to lead me to some sort of Nirvana. I simply knew I was called to be in this class and through Joli's influence and her advice, I let my mind be *open* - I wanted to *hear*. I let the lessons lead me and fought my innate desire to be in charge, the mindset I had lived for most of my life - the attitude that *I* knew what was best for *Me*. Through Joli, and with His grace, God opened my heart and called me to a higher level of spiritual growth.

Very quickly into the course we studied the topics of "why does God allow suffering" and "why do bad things happen." With Amber's death I never questioned my faith but I did struggle with *Why, if God was so powerful and can perform miracles, couldn't he have saved Amber? Why couldn't she have been on break, or why couldn't she have*

23

ducked underneath a desk, or why did an evil man shoot Amber in the first place? Why didn't God perform a miracle to save her life? At that time of my life I had no idea that anything as traumatic as Amber's death could happen to me or ever happen to me again. How wrong I was.

The book of Job is almost entirely related to the question: How can a good God allow suffering? I felt reassured to know that my questions of "why" were common questions regarding suffering. That God doesn't turn his back on miracles but it is for us to find something bigger in the suffering that we cannot see – that He can sometimes turn agony into ecstasy, or at least turn suffering into a revival that leads to new and better ways to approach life's challenges. That was a profound lesson for me. The cost of being human is that we have the ability to love, and the loss of a good and loving relationship is anguish – at least it was for me. I didn't take it lightly when I learned that we live in a world that is not meant to be permanent and with love comes suffering. Through Moms on Monday I was able to find peace in Amber's passing and even in the loss of Brecka's friendship. I knew we would be part of each other's life again but I finally understood that the constant of the lesson was working in its own way through Brecka and her family. And as for my family and me, we were all healing in our own way.

Joli explained early on in the course that she wanted us all to come to know God as a friend. This concept was not realistic to me: God as my friend? A friend is someone that I called on the phone, texted with, enjoyed company with during a lunch and exchanged gifts with on holidays. How could I have this same relationship with God? God was my creator, the One I regarded as my omnipotent guide, kind of like my personal Holy tour-guide through life, but I certainly did not regard our relationship as intimate personal friends. I questioned Joli, "How can God be your *friend*?" Joli explained that she learned through abiding in Christ that she started to develop a deeper relationship with God. "Abide," Joli said, "means to remain, to continue and stay or reside within. I want to be with God every day and have him as part of my being. It is a relationship that is always true." She painted a glorious picture of her relationship with God, and I too wanted God to abide in me.

As the weeks went on I worked to incorporate Christ-like thoughts and feelings into my daily life. The greatest lesson that impacted my family life was the lesson of *respect* in regard to relationships. I found that scripture reveals three clear elements that form the building blocks of all relationships: How people regard each other, how they respond to each other, and how they relate to each other. **Regard, Respond, and Relate.** When I got home that evening, after the kids were in bed and David was flipping channels on TV, I read the words from that lesson, "The first part of any relationship or friendship begins with three building blocks. Number One: An attitude of acceptance. Number Two: acting out of forgiveness. And Number Three: speaking the truth in love and serving out of love." I also re-read the paragraph on acceptance. "Our attitude of acceptance comes from trusting God. Acceptance is a major issue in marriage. Acceptance must be separated from approval of the other person's actions. Failure to accept your mate is one of the most destructive forces in marriage."

As I read these words I glanced over at David who had then found an episode of "Everybody Loves Raymond" and was laughing at the one-bit comical punch lines. I smiled as his laughter always brings me happiness. I thought of the expectations that I have held over him in our relationship. It was clear that some of my expectations were unrealistic. I tried my new way of thinking and our relationship began to grow over the coming weeks as I put these practices in place, without his knowing, and we became stronger as a couple. I began to see that much strife in our relationship came from my own unrealistic

expectations and I felt comforted in the fact that I could directly influence my ability to bring peace in our house.

My greatest growth in the course came through the lessons of prayer and learning how to pray. Joli started the lesson off with saying, "Nothing you can say will ever be more powerful than what you can pray."

Joli asked one of the group members to read the central idea written out in black and white on introductory pages of our lesson on prayer: "Prayer is the primary means by which God's will is to be achieved. It should be the primary way that we deal with everything in our lives. It is an incredible privilege God has given to us, and its power is limited only by the condition of our hearts. Our prayer life will be effective only when we are consistent in walking in light."

As the central idea was read out loud to the class I thought to myself, *OK, I know prayer is important. I pray when I need something and I pray for thanks for the blessings I receive.* I wasn't deeply impacted by the need to improve my praying skills. But then Joli added after the central idea was read, "Did you realize that there is effective prayer and ineffective prayer?" I thought, *Ineffective prayer?* My ears perked up. I never thought that I could be praying ineffectively.

I realized through our discussions, I had never learned the importance of prayer or even really how to pray. Prayers to me were more like rote recitals of nightly, or dinnertime prayers, or sometimes a prayer in pleading, "God, Get me out of this situation and I promise I will go to church every Sunday for the rest of my life."

I also didn't really pray a lot. Not that I didn't care, I just didn't know how important it truly was. If someone I knew lost a friend, I would say, "I am praying for you." But I really never *did* go pray for them. Again, not that I didn't care, but more thought that just saying "I am praying for you" was *like* praying, right? I would think about the person, but I never bowed my head or got on my knees and prayed.

As Joli continued the lesson, I outlined the three elements she discussed about effective prayer onto my notes worksheet: 1) Praying in faith. If we have faith in our hearts when we pray, God will respond. If we do not, we should not expect him to do so. 2) Praying with the correct motives. God does not respond to a person who is committed to self. He will respond to someone whose heart is committed to His will. 3) Pray in God's name, consciously relying on His power and authority and acting as his representative to see that his will is carried out.

I highlighted the following scripture that was referenced from the *New American Standard Bible*:

> (James 5: 13-18) Is anyone among you suffering? Let him pray. Is anyone cheerful? Let him sing praises. Is anyone among you sick? Let him call for the elders of the church, and let them pray over him, anointing him with oil in the name of the Lord. And the prayer offered in faith will restore the one who is sick, and the Lord will raise him up if he has committed sins; those sins will be forgiven. Therefore, confess your sins to one another, and pray for one another so that you may be healed. The effective prayer of a righteous man can accomplish much.

Prayer, effective prayer, became a regular part of my life and began to help me heal from the loss of Amber's life and Brecka's friendship, enrich my life and relationship with David, and provide strength for new adventures ahead.

CHAPTER TWO

A BEST
FRIENDSHIP

*A successful marriage
begins with a solid
friendship, a best friendship
and strengthens with
respect and love.*

David and I categorize ourselves as passionate businesspersons, maybe even better termed as serial entrepreneurs. We love business. We absolutely value family first but when we are not with our family, you will catch us working at our office, developing new business ideas together or probably watching Fox News Channel. In our marriage, we love working on projects together in business or even around the house and always do so with passion and enjoyment.

I met David in 1997 when working together as project managers for a construction company in Tulsa. It was a friendship at first encounter. I had just graduated from the University of Oklahoma with as BS in Construction Management and returned to Tulsa to work as a project manager for a commercial construction company. I was the first female project manager for the company – so uncommon for the firm that during my interview the company's owner said as he hiked his feet up on the desk, leaned back in his big leather chair and put his hands behind his head, "I have a secretary position open." I nearly walked out of his office right then but I knew management positions were limited in Tulsa and I needed a job. "I am actually applying for the management position." I came with high recommendations from a friend of his, a fact he began to recall as he scanned over my resume, "Oh, yeah – I heard about you."

I could definitely hold my own around the guys, always getting along better with men as friends throughout my life, but still I was nervous meeting the office team – all male with the exception of one other woman in the office – the secretary. While getting the office team introductions, David, who is six years my senior and had been with the company for five years, said, "I better watch out, you might be my boss someday." His humor immediately eased the tension of the new job and was so comforting that I took a stab back at him right away, "Yes, you better!"

When leaving OU I left behind my best friend and younger brother Aaron while he wrapped up school. Aaron and I always had so much fun together, just hanging out and talking about nothing. We coined most of our time together as our 'Seinfeld' moments. ("Seinfeld" – the 90's sitcom about four friends that would sit around laughing all day, basically talking about nothing.) As soon as David and I met, we instantly began spending work time together, talking and laughing about everything in general and nothing in particular, instant friends. I called Aaron that first week of my job to tell him how excited I was that I had found my 'Seinfeld' friend.

It wasn't long after David and I became friends and began hanging outside of the office that he suggested that we should go out on a date, *a real boyfriend and girlfriend date*. I pushed him away immediately and gave him the "let's be friends" line. That "let's be friends" line wasn't easy -- because I was attracted to him, we always had a blast together and he constantly made me laugh. But I didn't want to jeopardize the opportunity I was gaining in my construction management career.

Even after we had established the friends-only connection, we continued to hang out at work, after work, and even talking on the phone. Our friendship continued to grow rapidly and more and more deeply over those first few months. My career was growing rapidly as well.

David and I worked on my construction projects together. We complemented each other well in our jobs and enjoyed strategizing about projects. I also loved learning from him and admired his skill as an estimator, one aspect of the construction industry I just could never grasp.

By the time we had known each other for almost three months we were already nearly best-friend material. Of course the nice thing to do for your friends is to set them up on dates with other good friends. I set him up with one of my most adorable single friends, Sarah. David went with Sarah and I went with another guy I was casually dating at the time for dinner and drinks.

The double date took place at a popular restaurant and David and Sarah were getting along great. David even whispered to me when Sarah and my date were out of ear's reach, "she is really cute." We were all having a great time until David shared a funny story with the four of us from his work day about one of his subcontractors that had accidently backed his truck into a pond that was located on the jobsite and they spent the entire day towing his "dumb ass out." We all were in tears of laughter at the details of the story and in the moment David casually put his hand on

31

Sarah's shoulder touching her as a confirmation of the laughter they shared. I saw the touch and immediately was lost in thought as I realized he was flirting with her: *Hey, what are you doing? Get your hand off her!* It was a simple touch but he had been flirting with *me* over the past several months and now he wasn't flirting with me but with *Sarah!* It was an overreaction that made me realize right then and there on our double date – *Crap, I like him*.

The next day David and I had scheduled to hang out because, remember, we were best friends and hung out all the time. We ordered our beers and I drank fast, trying to get some courage up to tell him my big news:

"Um. I need to tell you something." I could hardly get the words out of my mouth. "Yes. What is it Adrienne?" David knew me well enough by then to know that it took quite a lot for me to be at a loss for words. He sensed it must be some sort of serious discussion.

I said, "Um..........I think I might like you." His witty answer was, "What do you mean, might?" I proceeded to tell him how uncomfortable it made me to watch him flirt with someone else the night before at dinner and that I really thought I liked him more than just being friends. I had no idea how he would take the news as he had been trying to get me to go out with him for months and with all my "let's be friends" he might be over the crush and ready to move on to someone else, perhaps Sarah.

It was quite the opposite. David was ecstatic about the idea of us as a couple and we decided to immediately start dating. We celebrated that night laughing, drinking and dancing all night and had our first kiss on the dance floor late that night. It was a kiss that felt perfect.

David and I always got along well and loved not only spending time together but doing everything together, including working together. We worked well as colleagues at my first job and were then, as now, a great balance in our skills. We enjoy each other's company in work so much so that even when we were very first dating we would talk about how fun it would be to start a business together. I come from a long line of entrepreneurs. My parents have been self-employed all of my life, currently operating a private investigation business, so owning a company was something that I had always thought about. We just didn't know that the opportunity to own our own company would come shortly after we started seriously dating.

My employer sent me to Meridian, Mississippi, as the project manager of a $4.5 million construction project – an amazing opportunity for a 23-year-old recent college graduate. My boss even razzed me that I wasn't old enough to rent a car but I was able to run his project. Despite my age, I did a great job on the project, bringing the job in on time and within schedule, even saving money for the owners. I even had a great time working with the good ol' boy contractors on the site too. They loved giving me a hard time but I respected them and their skills and they in turn respected me. All the while in Mississippi, I kept in close contact with David and our relationship, even though long-distance, grew serious very quickly.

My parents had scheduled a trip to come see me in Meridian towards the end of the project and were planning to arrive on Friday and stay through the weekend. My parents drive everywhere, no flying, due to my mom's aerophobia, so the drive would take all day Friday and they were to arrive around 9:00 p.m.

At around 6:30 p.m., while I was preparing to close up the job site for the night and lock the gates I got a call from my dad. My dad is always a jokester, so when I heard the chiming of his car's door-open warning in the background and his voice, "Mom is in the hospital, it is serious," I completely thought he was playing a joke on me.

"Come on in Dad, I know you are here in Mississippi, I can hear your car door chiming!"

"No, Adrienne, this is serious." My dad went on to tell me that Mom had an unexpected illness strike that morning and they didn't know what was going on but she was being admitted to St. John Hospital's Intensive Care Unit in Tulsa. In lieu of my parents visiting my jobsite that day I was back in Oklahoma less than seven hours after Dad's phone call.

When I arrived at St. John's Hospital in the early morning hours I was greeted by my dad, my older sister Merritt, my older brother Cameron, and David. I visited my mom briefly as she was hooked up to tubes and screaming in agony in room three of the ICU. The doctor summoned the immediate family into a small meeting room. Although David and I only had been dating for five months, no one in the family questioned David joining us as he had already become very close with our family.

The doctor said the last words I ever wanted to hear, "Your mother is not going to make it through the night." I froze as the doctor continued to talk and I could see his mouth moving but all I heard repeating in my head was *"not going to make it through the night."*

My youngest brother Aaron arrived shortly after the doctor's talk and he was filled in on the details. My dad explained that she had a rare muscle degeneration disease and there was no reason for the attack. They were performing more tests and attempting to get her stabilized. We prayed as a family, hugged one another and stayed by my mom's bedside until the nurses asked us to move into the waiting area. Gradually the rest of the family arrived, aunts and uncles and cousins, and friends. Throughout the evening we remained strong and prayed for a miracle.

Against the doctor's warning, miraculously my mom did make it through that night and through another few nights. One nurse told me, "The ICU is a place where people either stay three days and move into a regular room or they die here. It is a miracle your mom is still alive after a week."

After the first week she moved out of the ICU into a regular room. When the color started to return to her face, she could sit up on her own and was starting to heal, I knew that I had to return to work in Mississippi. My company was very helpful during that time and let me out of work with paid leave. They sent flowers and they never demanded that I return to work and told me to take as much time as I needed. But I knew that life must go on and my mom was even telling me the same. I returned to Meridian and left my mom and David behind.

David knew how hard it was for me to leave and I asked him to visit my mom if he could. I witnessed how much David loved me through the way he gave selflessly to my mom. David visited her every day for the first week I was gone and then continued to visit every few days, sharing selfless acts of giving up his evening to take her flowers rather than going out with friends, or stopping by during lunch to bring her a *Martha Stewart* Magazine rather than going to lunch with co-workers – anything to brighten her day. He called me after every visit to let me know how she was doing. They even developed a bond that is unique to mothers-in-law and sons-in-law. His actions were natural for David but made an impact on my heart forever.

After three months in the hospital, my mom continued her recovery at home and spent several months on dialysis getting her kidneys strong again. The illness weakened her heart, and her energy and strength diminished tremendously.

A few months after mom had returned home, I heard that my parents didn't know how they were going to continue the family business with my mom's strength waning. By that time David and I were engaged and started talking with each other about the idea of asking my mom to let David and me step in and help run their company. I have

grown up around the family, business helping as a young girl with filing in the office and as a teenager helping answer phones. But I had never trained to become an investigator or worked as an investigator for the company. Stepping into the business would mean learning a new trade, becoming a licensed private investigator, and giving up a lucrative job and rapidly growing career in the construction industry. We knew that there was risk but most importantly, my mom needed help.

We called my parents and proposed our idea. "Would you consider training me and selling the business to me?" There wasn't much convincing as my parents immediately loved the idea and we moved forward on plans to transition myself into the business. I moved back to Tulsa, quit my job and began to train as a licensed private investigator for Hide and Seek Investigations.

And it was such a fun and exciting business to learn. When my mom and dad started Hide and Seek in 1978 there was not the luxury of the Internet as a great resource and she learned investigations the old fashioned way. She loves the vast resources the Internet has allowed but always stresses that it is so important to go above and beyond what you can find online – the personal touch – and how to gather all the pieces of the puzzle and pull the information together to develop the full picture. I listened and learned and soaked in all of her investigating secrets. She is a brilliant woman and I appreciated her mentorship in my education for a new career.

As my first up-close encounter with death, I saw how final death would be, how hers could have been. Since the time that my mom almost died, I felt like I was given a gift of a lifetime. The gift was a second chance to know my mom, work with her, learn a new profession and most importantly spend time laughing together – time that shouldn't have been. But then again it was perhaps entirely according to God's plan as that second chance would steer the course of David's and my life forever.

Experiencing LOVE

CHAPTER THREE

BRAND NEW
BUSINESS

Building a business with your spouse can be one of the most rewarding experiences in your life, but also perhaps one of the most challenging. Stay focused on the goal.

When I was little I wasn't the typical girl that played with Barbies or cabbage patch dolls – I had dreams of owning my own business. I had been told the story throughout my life that when I was three and my grandfather asked what I wanted to be when I grew up, I answered with all seriousness, "I want to tell people what to do." That is what I thought business people did.

I was excited to have the opportunity to become a

business owner at the age of 25! Being a fearful-of-everything person, I came to learn that in business it was one of the places that I had almost no fears.

I took David on the journey with me. He wasn't a born entrepreneur or a risk-taker. He appreciated having the steady paycheck but at the same time liked the idea of controlling his destiny through owning our own business. But the balance is what has made us a great team. I say, *Let's jump off the cliff*, and David says, *Whoa, let's measure the drop, check our parachutes and review the weather*.

Even though David was part of Hide and Seek's growth through advice and support, he wasn't involved in the day to day operations of the business and we soon learned that we significantly missed working together. Although Hide and Seek was a perfect supplemental income for our family, unfortunately it didn't have the capacity to support our entire family's financial needs. We realized that David must continue his job, having been promoted to Vice President of another construction firm.

Our desire to work together kept us constantly thinking of different businesses that we could start so that we could produce an income that would support our family. And then we had a *Big Idea*.

With our business needs and family needs (three-year-old Canaan and one-year-old Ethan), we were in constant struggle to find childcare around our chaotic schedule. As an investigator I needed care for four hours here and there and it was typically at the last minute as my schedule changed weekly. I had to work around the client's needs (mostly attorneys) so I often found myself having to run out to a courthouse when I had planned a day in with the kids.

I reached out to our local daycares, which required full-time contracts. I also reached out to our local nanny services who stated that they couldn't help us unless we utilized twenty-plus hours per week with a regular standing request. We settled on paying for the daycare full-time but needing it as-is. That scenario quickly became an inconvenience to our family but mainly to the daycare. They didn't appreciate me popping in and out during the day while they had ongoing activities with other students.

My first thought was to hire the preschool teacher from Canaan's class directly for our flexible needs. We felt we could pay her enough to work for us throughout the week to keep her employed directly for us. But first before offering her the job I wanted to run a more in-depth background screening on her. I knew from my experience with the state's criminal screening required by the daycares and schools that government criminal record keeping for public access is, in the very least, lacking in efficiency and thoroughness. For example a disclaimer on the state's criminal reporting website states, "If the fingerprint card was not submitted or the fingerprints were not retained because of poor quality, we will not have a record."

I performed a general public record screening on the teacher, gathering records that are accessible to a licensed private investigator and that do not require employee authorization to obtain. Immediately I began finding negative records on his teacher that sent chills down my spine. *This woman has been watching my child?* I first identified a domestic suit against the teacher and her family in which a protective order was filed and granted. Following that, the teacher filed a protective order against the opposing party. There was never a dismissal of the case. The details of the matter stated that an assault was made by the teacher and the matter was less than six months previous to the initial filing. *During the time Canaan was attending her class!*

I also identified two eviction notices in her name. One notice was as recent as five months prior to my research. No telling where she was living at this point. Probably back with the family that she had filed assault

41

charges against. People involved in matters of several altercations with family members typically don't break the cycle and I didn't want my kids in the presence of a woman with history of strife, fiduciary irresponsibility and who knows what else.

It was shocking that our state background screening didn't identify these important safety and character matters in regards to the teacher that I was leaving my firstborn with on a weekly basis.

After sharing the news with David, we decided to immediately pull the boys immediately out of school and we had to start finding another solution for our family so that I could get some work done. We started compiling a list of babysitters that could work for us here and there. I performed a screening on all of them and we utilized our own sitters as needed.

We had no idea that we had a business in the making until our 2004 summer travels. Just weeks after compiling our in-house babysitter list, managing sitter engagements successfully for ourselves, family, and friends, we took two back-to-back trips to Denver and Austin. We had no luck finding sitters during either trip but it was in Austin, Texas where our Big Idea materialized. We went from wondering "why doesn't this service exist anywhere?!" to "let's do it ourselves!"

After a week of family time with relatives, with activities at the water park and children's museum - kids crawling on us every waking moment - we were looking forward to our one adult night out on our last evening with my brother Cameron and sister-in-law, Traci. Our plans were quickly thrown into a chaotic tail spin when we had to find a last minute back-up sitter as the scheduled sitter bailed on us to see a concert. (Who hasn't had this happen?!)

Traci quickly found the back-up babysitter list from the neighborhood association directory and we all grabbed our cell phones and started calling the over thirty listed babysitters. After calling every last one of them, the only possible candidate (nearly the only one that answered the phone) was a fourteen-year-old boy down the street. "What is your babysitting experience?" I asked. He answered unassertively, "Well, I have a younger brother that I watch a lot." And the fact that he was fourteen left us with no ability to perform any type of background screening. Not that it was necessarily at the top of our minds that this fourteen-year-old was a juvenile criminal offender, but it's not possible to do a background check on a teen so if we had felt like checking up on him, there wouldn't have been any way to do it. No references were listed for any of these sitters.

Needless to say, David and I didn't get to go out that night and pouted through every poopy diaper change, imagining the laughter, yummy food and spit-up-less dinner we could be enjoying.

After hugs and kisses to the family the next morning, we drove up to Oklahoma. During the drive we couldn't stop talking about how disappointed we were that we didn't get to have our adult night out and that there should be a business like this - safe babysitters, on-call and experienced - for parents in distress!

We had so much fun brainstorming the idea in the car and jotting down ideas, we quickly formed a back-of-the-envelope business plan.

Throughout the drive, we thought about how we could together create a national online sitter-service that provided the extensive background screening that I had done on our sitters, using the research techniques I had learned as an investigator. David even thought of a name: SeekingSitters. We looked at each other with the same thoughts in our head: *Should we do this? Could we really do this? Are we crazy?* We spent the next few hours of the drive in silence while moving our thoughts from fun, pie-in-the-sky planning to the reality of budgets, marketing and

website programming. By the time we had made it within an hour of our home we had decided to give it a go. We wrote down a list of to-dos to take care of when we got home to get this sitter-service off the ground and the first to-do was to set up the website. We got home and unloaded the bags from the trip, unpacked the kids and pulled out the laptop to see if the seekingsitters.com website name was available – and it was! Ten minutes later and we had a brand new business that we were starting together.

We were so ecstatic about the potential of this business, as maybe it would be our opportunity to allow us the privilege to work together and for me to spend my days with my best friend again.

CHAPTER FOUR

LIFE HAPPENS

There are some things in your life you will have no control over. In these times you pray. Your outcome at times may not be as you would have thought, but rather how God has intended.

We began development of our new company, SeekingSitters, while continuing the investigation business and even continuing to grow our family. Little did we know that we were pregnant with our third on the way home from our Austin trip, and a few months later we found out that our boys would have a little sister arriving the following summer.

The business grew quickly, requiring David to help more and more. He would do billing in the evenings while I

completed sitter investigations and took care of the kids. During the days while he headed off to his construction job, I would drive around town (sometimes with my kids in tow) visiting businesses and introducing our unique online sitter-service to the Tulsa area and basically anyone who would listen.

David was excited about the business and its success in Tulsa but he was also skeptical of building it on a grand scale; therefore he proposed to test it in a second market in Oklahoma City. Immediately we saw growth. But what we learned from that second location was that we were unable to manage it remotely and began to look into franchising as an option for growth. We sought out advisors to ask about the viability of our business in the franchising arena and we were told that our model couldn't work in franchising. The naysayers did not discourage David and me but were rather just one of the many challenges we would come to face together, conquer, and move along our path as husband and wife/father and mother entrepreneurs.

We set out to franchise our business on our own. We researched all we could, found a great franchise attorney, started developing documents and prayed a lot. And God did answer our prayers sooner than we could have imagined. Before we even finished our franchise documents in the summer of 2006, we got a call from a prospective husband and wife buyer of our Oklahoma City location. They had recently been stood up by their babysitter and the father was so frustrated about the situation that he had a vision of starting a Merry Maids type service for babysitters. When he told his wife the idea she said, "That is ridiculous." The very next day a story ran in their paper about our company and how SeekingSitters was looking to franchise and the Oklahoma City location was for sale. He was stunned to see what he had imagined not only did exist in his area, but the company was for sale! He showed the article to his wife, and after she read it she said, "That is brilliant!" Soon after they became our first franchise location.

We kept moving forward and by 2007, SeekingSitters had grown to five franchises and the Tulsa franchise location was doing enough in sales that David was able to leave his job in December that year. We had found success in our business and we had met our goal of finding a career where we could be together and afford our family's needs and we were nervous and excited with the thrill of business accomplishment that only an entrepreneur can know.

But what we didn't realize is that during the first week of working together we would worry that we had made the worst mistake of our lives.

♡ ♡ ♡

When David came on board full-time with me (during actual day-time work hours), we moved into a small commercial building in Tulsa, so small that David and I had to share one of the larger offices to make room for our assistant, the investigator, and office manager in the other three offices. That first week after moving in we began working together filling babysitting jobs, answering the phones and handling customers' needs. I had been running  SeekingSitters by myself (but pleading for more help) for the past two years and now that *he* was in the mix it was interrupting my rhythm. We were stepping on each other's feet constantly, figuratively and literally, in that small office! By the end of the week our constant arguments ended in my demand, "Is there any way you can get your old job back?" At that frustration point we stopped arguing and we both remembered: *This is what we wanted, to work together!* We knew we had to figure out a way to make it work, and we had to figure it out fast. We began a plan to divide tasks, separate roles, and move offices. No more stepping on toes and each other's feelings!

After that we learned to work well through challenges *together* and the more we learned about working together in business, the more it seemed to strengthen our marriage. First and foremost we were friends and we loved to talk about business. We have never had rules about when to talk about business or not talk about business. If we wanted to talk about it at dinner, we did. If the day was stressful we didn't. We had great communication and could debate a topic but then turn it off and focus our attention on our family. We also never made a decision where one of us was completely on one side and the other on another side. We would always come to a decision that we could both agree upon.

Our company became part of the family as well. As soon as they were capable of understandable pronunciation, our kids would answer the home phone, "SeekingSitters, may I help you." And the kids loved meeting the new sitters. Canaan had heard our sitter orientation so many times that even at five years old when a sitter would come to the house he would say, "Let me tell you how it works."

We have great fun working together but when I tell people that I work with my husband, their first reaction is surprise and then one of two responses: "Wow, I could never do it!" or "How do you do it?" The shock that I receive from people who don't understand how we can work together actually strikes me as odd. Nowadays it's perceived as an anomaly for husbands and wives to work together as one in a business venture. Since 1975 my parents have worked together, my aunt and uncle work together in business, and even David's parents worked together for over 40 years on the family farm. A once common way of life has become such an anomaly.

That is not to say every day is easy-peasy and we always get along. We definitely have our days that we work very hard not to lose our temper at each other in front of our employees, and have the patience and respect to save our grievances for when we're home behind closed doors. I have to ask myself, *would I talk like that to another person in the office - no way! Would we argue a business matter in front of our children - no way!*

These moments in the office pale in comparison to some of the stresses we had already experienced as a married couple. When we built our home we chose to do the contracting ourselves in lieu of hiring a builder, utilizing our skills and connections in the construction industry. The stress it caused on our young marriage was a first test of the marriage vow, "till death do us part," because the project nearly killed us. Sheetrock dust covering every surface in the house, daily hunting for items through half unpacked boxes, spending days working our paying jobs and doing some physical construction work ourselves in the evening hours.

I don't remember the fight, if there was a fight, or if it was just the culmination of a day or a week of sheer stress. I was in the upstairs hallway of the half-way finished house, holding our eighteen-month-old and pregnant with our second, crying uncontrollably, telling David I was leaving. David sat down next to me and said, "I am not letting you." We talked through the night and decided to work together to pull our life back on track. (Step one: finish the construction project! Step two: invent a babysitting company and start going on date nights!) Through our

commitment to each other, we made it through and felt like we could tackle anything in our marriage!

But during the spring of 2009 we experienced more stressful times: Three children under the age of six and running three separate rapidly growing companies. The franchise system had expanded to thirty five locations and the franchisees were growing with amazing success. The local owners as well as the franchise system received media attention and accolades for our growth. An appearance on CNBC "The Big Idea with Donny Deutsch", *Working Mother Magazine* national award, and in late August 2009 CNN Headline News aired a feature story on SeekingSitters.

David and I were handling it all, but it was so hard on us that we were slowly losing the happiness in our lives. Stress took its toll on us and we spent the summer with constant chaos in our relationship, our children, our life, our business. We bootstrapped the businesses, so money was limited and all the pressures were on our shoulders. We started taking the stress out on each other, as you tend to take it out on the ones you love.

Looking back, it is really simple to see why that time seemed unbearable to us, as we were backwards in our priorities. We spent our every waking moment dedicated to the business. We have stringent work ethics, had and always will, but around that time there were some days that we were not even available to our family or to ourselves. We teach our franchisees that the culture of our business is "Family First" on their first day of training and we weren't following our own culture.

The stress had gone on for months and we knew we had to fix it – together, rather than continuing to work against each other. *We are a team!* We had to remember that by working together we could make our lives orderly and peaceful.

Most importantly, we realized that God had taken a back seat to our business growth and our family growth.

What I had adopted in my prayer habits many years earlier moved from daily to sometimes. To heal, we turned to the footing of our relationship: our faith.

We began attending church regularly, which quickly became my favorite time of the week. A quiet time away from the children and business where I could absorb the sermon, drift into thoughts of how each lesson related to our life, and simply sit next to David, holding his hand.

We started praying individually and praying together: *God, Help us, deliver us from this frustration and give us peace. Help us with our children. Help us find support in our office. Help us in our relationship.*

The remarkable thing was that as we kept praying we slowly began to heal. We had forgotten to keep God as an integral part of our life. Our existence focused solely on growing our business and we were missing what was important in holding us together. Once we got God back in our lives, we began to heal.

We also remembered to give attention to our relationship. We own a babysitting service, we have sitters at our disposal, and we had forgotten to have a Date Night! We had to start changing our habits and working at making peace in our home. We always believed that our love as husband and wife is only superseded by God, but we had forgotten our commitment to this promise. We had to be reminded that we, under God, needed to put each other first, over business, children and friends. When we started putting each other first again we began to see our relationship renew itself and once more Love was what mattered most. Our faith and prayers helped us remember what really is important in life and that through prayer and with God's grace we can overcome any **obstacle**.

We began to realize our life was a wonderful and blessed chaos and we found happiness in that – happiness isn't something that we are entitled to have, it had to be seized and nurtured. Not that the stresses of work went

away, we just learned how to find a better perspective, balance our life and take a break every once in a while.

We became more sensitive to our expectations for one another – not to assume that we are completely alike in how we handle each situation. We both learned how to recognize each other's strengths and accept support in our weaknesses.

We began practicing these relationship building blocks: Acceptance, Love and Forgiveness. Most of all, we never gave up on *us*. Our relationship grew stronger and by the end of September 2009 we had overcome the temptations of giving way to anger and frustration and built a foundation of faith for ourselves and our children.

In October David and I were a team again. We felt we had a handle on nurturing and guiding our family, we had the help we needed in our business, and most importantly, we had each other.

Experiencing LOVE

CHAPTER FIVE

FALL AT
THE FARM

God intervened. He nudged us home a day early from a relaxing weekend at The Farm. He knew we needed to be close to home.

Fall break is a favorite time to go to The Farm. October is harvest time at David's family's spread in Columbus, Nebraska, and the kids enjoy spending their entire weekend picking corn and riding on the combine with Uncle Steven. These activities are far from our life in the city, where our idea of growing vegetables consists of tomatoes in a pot, which end up dying halfway through the summer season because no one has had time to water them.

We knew that an impromptu getaway to The Farm for the holiday break would be perfect timing to leave behind our day-to-day worries, to relax and reflect on our newly-realized approach to relieving stresses in our life. The

great advantage of self-employment is that you can get up and go at the spur of the moment and these fall-time visits to The Farm have become part of our family tradition. For that October 2009 trip, it was a typical weekend on the farm: relaxing in front of the TV; our daughter playing dress-up in the basement; the boys in the field hand-picking corn.

The farmhouse sits on a quarter section (one hundred sixty acres) of David's ancestors' land, amidst thousands of fertile acres of Nebraska soil that was the center of the proverbial "Breadbasket of the World." The original house, constructed in the 1950s, was rebuilt in 1987, with an old barn in the back and two newer barns on each side of the house. David's mom and dad lived on and farmed the land all their lives. The Farm was part of David's life as well. The youngest of the seven children, David spent his afterschool hours and summers in the corn fields helping plant and harvest.

David's faith in God was also an integral part of his life on the farm. Just a quarter mile down the country road was Zion Lutheran church where his parents were married, where David was baptized, where they spent every Sunday morning with his family, and where his dad was buried a few years ago.

The Kallweit family had suffered two unexpected deaths in the first few years of our marriage. David's father died in a farming accident, occurring during our honeymoon and halting our celebratory vacation. Although a newcomer to the Kallweits, I recognized his passing was a deep loss for the family. A few years later, David's eldest sister, Bonnie, died of cancer. I had only known Bonnie for a few short years but she impacted my life in a special way. I admired her family values and the love she gave her three boys. She was so proud of each of them. She told me once when I was tired and strained with my young children, "These are the best times of your life. Cherish them." I will never forget her gentle nature and I keep a handwritten note from her in my bible next to my bed.

Since his father's passing, David's mom has managed the farm estate. She is the backbone of the Kallweit clan - mother of seven, 13 times a grandmother and twice a great-grandmother. David's mom is absolutely the most resourceful person I know and I have always admired her. Raised on a farm, she learned early how to make something out of nothing. She's told us stories about how she made her own dolls and toys when she was growing up. (I even witnessed this one Christmas when I saw her take the plastic packaging encasing a toy, save it, and later used it as a fun art activity for the kids.) In her garden, she grows much of the family's food and has the best homemade jelly in the world, bar none. Her jelly and jam are as precious as gold. When we are lucky enough to get a few jars to take home to Catoosa I hide them from the kids, to use ONLY on special occasions. One time back home the kids accidentally knocked an entire jar off the counter, shattering the entire contents onto the floor. All three kids instantaneously screamed in anguish, as if our pet dog had just died. They wanted to scoop it up, saying with remorse, "We can save it, Mom!"

We left Catoosa for holiday trip on Thursday and had planned a Monday morning return since school was out. But for no reason in particular, towards the end of the visit we decided to change our plans and leave a day early. The kids were not happy about the news as they love being at The Farm. Canaan even questioned us, "Why do we have to go home from the farm early?" and after I replied "Daddy and I have to get home to work." Canaan had a long pause and said perceptively, "You own the company, don't you?"

We hit the road back early mid-afternoon for our drive home, planning a past-bedtime arrival. The entire seven-hour drive was trouble-free. The kids were calm and respectful towards David and me and we felt like all the past month's hard work and prayer had come together. We were proud of ourselves, like we wanted to give each other a high-five for peace in our life, in our kids, even in the car. It was an overall great weekend and an aura of happiness prevailed as we traveled from Nebraska to Oklahoma.

As soon as we arrived home and put the kids to bed, we reflected on the weekend. I sat up in our bed exclaiming, "David, I am so happy that we are a team. It makes all the difference in everything. Relaxing at The Farm was the perfect 'time-out' to get re-energized." The break did seem to give us a zest for moving forward. Our attitude towards life was filled with motivation, excitement for our business and love for each other as we sat up in bed talking about business plans for the week ahead.

We then began to discuss David's mother before we fell asleep. David said that he had felt some distress for her over the weekend as she seemed unhappy. "I worry about my mom. I wish I could be there more often, to be with her." Imagining the loss that she had suffered since his dad passed away and especially after Bonnie died was impossible. I admired his mother, her strength and grace and we both wanted nothing more than to understand a way to help relieve her sorrow.

Contemplating death, we began discussing what would happen if one of us died. "I can't imagine what it would be like if you died. I don't know what I would do without you." David responded, "I would want you to remarry. I never want you to be alone." I told him that I would want him to remarry as well and trying to relieve the serious tone, "At least wait a few months, OK?!"

It didn't feel sad to talk about the subject of dying and how we would hypothetically move on with our life, just like a topic we needed to be discussing. We went to bed, suitcases on the floor still unpacked.

CHAPTER SIX

ONE UP ME

Good and bad things simply happen in life. These facts must be accepted. It is important to keep calm and surround yourself with support and faith, and from that, strength will come.

September 11, 2001, 9/11. A day when an attack on our nation caused chaos on the streets, confusion for the faithful, and changed the way life had been forever. However, September 11th is actually a day of celebration for David and me. It is the day that we got married in 1999. Every year we celebrate September 11th.

October 19, 2009 is our 9/11.

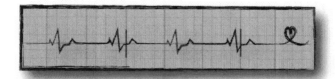

Throughout our marriage it always seemed that when I was sick, David *coincidentally* would get sick just a couple of days later, sometimes simultaneously. If I complained my head hurt, his head started hurting just a little bit worse. If I had a cold, the next day he had the flu. It became so ridiculous that I would give him a hard time about it. I always said it was his way of trying to one-up me. I even once made up feeling sick just to test if it was a real condition of his, to one-up me. (He did get "mysteriously sick" just a few days later.)

I am not sure if it was a natural reaction to seek out the sympathy from me, or if it was that he didn't want to have to take care of me when I was sick. But in any case, David's "play-possum" act was more comical than annoying.

The morning after returning from The Farm the alarm went off at 7:00 a.m. to get everyone moving and ready for the sitter we scheduled for 10:00 a.m. As the alarm went off, I felt a little sick to my stomach and said to David, "I'm not feeling well. I am sure nothing serious but I'm going to sleep in just a bit longer." Being the drill sergeant that he is in the morning, his non-response to my "please let me sleep in" told me that he was unhappy that I didn't jump up with him right away. I stayed in bed and rested and David started brushing his teeth.

From the bathroom I heard David gagging. Gagging is a mild expression to explain the noise my husband makes when the coughs or gags. The force from his body is so great that I have learned over the years the warning signs that he displays when he is about to cough so I can prepare myself by plugging my ears with my fingers as if a bomb is about to erupt.

Hearing David gagging, I didn't jump up immediately. Not only was the sound always exaggerated, it was a pretty regular occurrence for David to start gagging on his toothbrush. There must be a condition for this toothbrushing-gag-itis, because I have even heard of others suffer from the intrusion of the toothbrush in their mouths. So I didn't think anything serious of it, but I did immediately think: *OK, here he goes one-upping me again! Since I just said I felt sick, he starts throwing up.*

I shouted to the bathroom, "You trying to one-up me?" while laughing softly to myself. He didn't answer me. I repeated louder, "David, you trying to one-up-me?" and then he answered back with his voice shaking, "Adrienne, help."

The next thing I knew I was in the bathroom. I think my body must have levitated there because I don't remember physically getting out of the bed or opening the doors to the bathroom. But I remember arriving in front of him to see his body underneath his pedestal sink, face down, shaking. When I reached him, he looked straight up at me but his eyes were glazed like a newborns as if he saw but didn't comprehend what he was seeing. He said in an unsteady and shivering-like voice, "I think I am having a seizure."

I am not a nurse, but because of our babysitting service, I keep my CPR and First Aid up to date and had some knowledge of what signs to look for in a seizure.

"David, look at me." He could look me in the eyes. I thought: *This is a good sign.*

"How many fingers am I holding up?"

He could see and count my fingers, "Three."

"What is your name?"

"David Kallweit." As he answered, his body was limp and he remained crouched under the sink but he became somewhat more alert and could focus on me though I could see in his eyes he was confused. Even as he looked at me, he continued to slowly creep his body further under the sink and towards the wall. I knew something was not right, but my first thought was that he had gotten up too fast from his toothbrushing-gag-itis and the blood rushed to his head, making him lightheaded.

"Call an ambulance," he said affirmatively but in a feeble voice. David is 6'1" and nearly 225 pounds and lifting him up from the floor was not an option. "David, crawl to the carpet and lie down, I will call for help." On his hands and knees with me following beside, David crawled to the bedroom and as he neared the bed he said he wanted to lie down. I helped him take hold of the bed and he was able to assist himself enough to climb up. I asked him how he was feeling and he said that he was dizzy and "something didn't seem right." He couldn't fully explain the odd feeling and didn't complain of any pain but just knew that something was not right with his head and began to rub it with his hand.

I called our office manager, Christina, to try getting a babysitter to the house sooner than we had scheduled. We live thirty miles from a hospital and it would be faster to drive David to the emergency room myself than wait for an ambulance.

By that time Canaan was awake and came into our room. "What is going on?"

"Canaan, this is very serious. Please go to your room and make sure your brother and sister stay in their rooms. Daddy is very sick." Canaan is by nature very inquisitive and always needs to know more but the tone in my voice didn't leave room for questions. Canaan knew it was serious and followed my instructions immediately.

With school out and slim chances on getting a sitter out to the house within the hour, we needed to find a solution for the kids so I could get David to town immediately. The next call I made was to David's sister who lives in Tulsa about twenty minutes from our house. She didn't pick up so I left a message: "Carol, something is wrong with David. Can you please come out here so I can take him to the hospital?"

I told David to lay his head back and rest his eyes and I sat next to him. Less than a minute later his sister returned my call and said she would make arrangements to get out to our house immediately. While I was talking to her David sat up in the bed but I noticed that he continued to rub his head. I got off the phone and told him she was on her way. He said in a weak voice but much more clearly than earlier, "I'm feeling better. I don't think we need to go to the emergency room but I do want to go see the doctor."

The next call was to Dr. Michelle Kelley, our family physician. "I need to bring David in. He just passed out in our bathroom and is complaining of a really bad headache." Dr. Kelley's nurse was helpful, "We can get him in at 10:00 a.m." *Thank God*, I thought.

David seemed to be doing better so much so that he got out of bed and took a shower. The fact that he took a shower and was moving around and talking put all of us at ease, thinking nothing too serious must be going on. I got the kids situated with breakfast so that I could get ready myself. I put on my typical work shoes for the day, 2" heels, but while turning off the lights in the closet for some reason I felt drawn back to change shoes. I grabbed a pair of flat shoes that I had actually put in a bag to give away. That simple task was almost like God nudging me, *You have a long day ahead of you, get a bit more comfortable, Adrienne.*

David had moved to the downstairs couch and was lying down doing some work from his smartphone. Around 9:15 a.m. his sister arrived. Shortly after her arrival he said his head was beginning to hurt, describing a headache, dizziness, and the feeling of blood rushing so loud he could hear it in his ears. The pain intensified rapidly, so much so

that he said, "Let's go. I need to go now." David stood up and as he headed out the door stopped to hug each of the kids, tell them he loved them and reminded them to be good for their Aunt Carol. He gave Carol a hug and a kiss and we left for the doctor.

During our drive to the doctor I gave David a hard time about having to one-up me, "So you know this is all about one-upping me. As soon as I said I wasn't feeling well, you started gagging and not feeling well." He laughed. "Really, I know something is going on, but you know you just had to one-up me!" He laughed even harder but immediately started complaining that his head hurt too much to laugh.

I tried to keep the mood light and continued to try to cheer him up and not worry about what was going on. I reminded him of the conversation the night before about dying and getting old and said, "I hope this isn't a sign of our old age to come where we complain of our ailments all the time." Again he laughed harder and then complained again, "Ouch, that hurts to laugh." He kept saying his head hurts and the pain quickly got more and more intense. I got the hint and stopped the jokes and told him to rest his head.

I tried to ease his worry and said that even though I was aware something was not right, I was sure he would be OK.

We checked into the doctor's office and David immediately asked if the receptionist could turn off the lobby room TV as the sound was "killing his head." *The TV too loud in the waiting area – that was odd?* That was the first significant sign that something was serious. Before I could even finish the check-in procedure David asked if he could go into a room to lie down. Dr. Kelly had been our family doctor for years. The staff knows David well enough that when he asked to lie down, they took him seriously and immediately led us into an exam room.

At that point everything became a whirl of intense

and deliberate action, people moving so fast that I could hardly keep up with what was going on with David.

The nurse came in the room with a bowl and immediately David started gagging and throwing up in it. Dr. Kelley rushed into the room and began rubbing anti-nausea medicine on David's hip. Another nurse entered the room. Dr. Kelley and the two nurses and I surrounded David as he lay in agony.

They handed me a towel to cool his face. I stood next to him, holding his head as he threw up more and more, all over himself, my shoes, the room. Then all Hell broke loose. I don't use the cliché lightly. I mean it literally, all Hell broke loose. He looked up at me, right in my eyes, with an "I'm scared" look, closed his eyes and then started throwing up again.

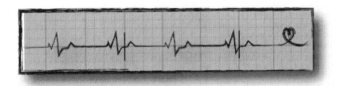

The vomiting stopped and immediately his body went into an uncontrollable fit. I didn't know what I was witnessing. The immediate thought was, *My husband is dying in my arms.* I screamed frantically through the doctor's office. "OH MY GOD! OH MY GOD! SOMEONE HELP ME! SOMEONE HELP ME!" I blacked out for a moment as I was screaming; I was out of my body, hearing myself scream. Seeing the catastrophe from this perspective, I could hear the desperation in my own voice. I felt completely out of control.

At the moment of my scream, more of Dr. Kelley's staff rushed into David's room and hovered over him. No one was talking or explaining anything. It was just a frenzy of calculated actions to save David. I thought I was losing my husband, my best friend forever. My thoughts didn't go much deeper than that and I felt out of control. I closed my eyes with my head bowed over David and prayed: *God, Help David.* I didn't know what else to pray because I didn't know what was wrong. I just prayed for David and for God to be there with us. As soon as I asked God for help, a sense of peace and strength came over me and suddenly He took control and it helped me handle the situation with my head rather than my heart.

I thought back to my CPR training and started noting David's symptoms. Wild thrashing movements from his legs and upper torso, his eyes rolling back in his head, and a constricting tongue. I recognized he must be having a seizure. *Oh, God, why was I so blasé this morning in the bathroom when he thought he was having a seizure.* Only seconds after the violent thrashing began, his body state altered into complete rigidness and slow pulsing movements. His eyes closed and his tongue continued constricting. I rubbed his head with the wet towel to prevent it from falling off the table. His tongue was blocking his air passage as he gasped, almost gurgling, for air.

I was so scared that he couldn't breathe. "David, you need to breathe, honey. David, you need to breathe," I kept repeating over and over while stroking the cold wet wash cloth on his head.

The doctor and nurses moved through the series of events as if they had prepared for the drill a hundred times. Later I would learn that David's extreme condition was the first time they had put into use a "Code Blue" type of urgent resuscitation on a patient. I followed their lead in standing by David's side, waiting out the episode.

As his body movements began to completely calm and the seizure waned, Dr. Kelley explained what was going on. "David just had a seizure and he is now in the postictal state, the period following the seizure. He is breathing and we have oxygen on him. An ambulance will be here soon and they will take him to the hospital to determine what is going on." "Ok." All I could muster while still shaking from the entire experience. The activity in the room faded into the background as I kept my focus on David. I kept the towel on his head and kept stroking his hair. I whispered into his ear, "Everything is going to be OK." I continued praying.

These two minutes changed my life forever and David doesn't remember any of it.

Experiencing LOVE

CHAPTER SEVEN

GETTING THE
DIAGNOSIS

God will speak to you
if you pray and then
listen. The listening is
the key. Those whispers
are not to be ignored.

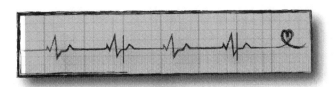

About seven minutes after the seizure began, six firemen and an ambulance with a team of medics arrived at Dr. Kelley's office. Due to their timing, they obviously had been called by Dr. Kelley's staff during the onset of the seizure. As soon as the firemen walked into the patient room, the nurses were relieved to see them and knew them by name. Lifting David onto the stretcher and into the

Experiencing L O V E

ambulance was going to take strength and Dr. Kelley's office staff's reassuring acceptance of the firemen immediately showed me that they would take care of David. We all moved out of their way and I grabbed my phone to text Christina at the office.

Adrienne:
Get hold of Carol 911. 911 We are going to St. John David just had a seizure

Christina:
I'm calling her now

The firemen and medic team moved David from the bed in the doctor's office to the ambulance gurney still in the postictal state; his body was completely dead weight. It took all six firemen to move him to the gurney.

As the firemen wheeled David through the front door, he woke up and pulled his hands up towards his head, indicating he was still in pain. The firemen were talking to him, "David we are taking you to the ambulance." David didn't respond.

I said goodbye to Dr. Kelley and her office team and hugged a few of them, "Thank you." Dr. Kelley asked me to keep her updated on how he is doing and I followed David on the gurney out towards the parking lot.

The tall, very tough looking female medic (let's call her Charlie because with all the commotion I wouldn't have remembered her name even if she told me) was in charge of the direction and ambulance ride to St. John. "I need you to fill out this paperwork," she said as she handed the forms to sign just as if David had a minor bruise and we had all the time in the world. "We need your consent to treat David since he can't sign these – you have to sign them." I wanted to scream at the top of my lungs: *ARE YOU KIDDING! MY HUSBAND JUST ALMOST DIED IN MY ARMS AND JUST A FEW MINUTES AGO ALL YOU CARE ABOUT IS HAVING ME SIGN THESE STUPID FORMS. START THE AMBULANCE, TURN ON THE LIGHTS AND LET'S GET TO THE EMERGENCY ROOM.* I worked furiously to sign everything they needed as they hooked David up to morphine, a blood pressure cuff and monitors and strapped him into the ambulance for the ride.

David became semi-conscious as they got him situated in the ambulance but he still had not opened his eyes and continued to complain about the pain. It was radiating throughout his head and increasing in intensity. We had no idea of the seriousness ahead of us but began to relax some because he was talking, asking for pain medicine and moving his arms and legs.

He kept asking Charlie for pain medicine as the morphine hadn't kicked in yet. I asked Charlie to please give him the medicine and she abrasively replied, "Hon, we have so much medicine in there he is going to sleep the entire ride to the hospital. It will just take a minute to kick in." I became more and more concerned because David was in agony and instead of sitting with him and hugging him and telling him that he would be at the hospital soon, I had to finish filling out the required paperwork. I scribbled my signature on all the paperwork and thrust it in Charlie's hand. She told me to follow the ambulance to the hospital in my vehicle.

I jumped out of the ambulance and headed towards David's Ford Expedition (we call the truck), the only vehicle we had available that day. I hate David's truck. I swear it was one of the Hurricane Katrina casualties and re-sold in Oklahoma to unsuspecting Midwestern buyers because the thing always reeks like old tennis shoes or dog vomit. Every time I get into the truck my body immediately goes into an obstinate mode like a balking horse that refuses to get into the starting gate. Having to drive his truck at that instant made a stressful moment even more intense. I heard the ambulance doors shut behind me as I realized I didn't have David's truck keys. Looking through the truck window, I had accidently locked the keys in the truck when we arrived at the doctor. I immediately changed direction and ran towards the ambulance that had just begun to inch out of the parking lot.

The driver spotted me running towards the ambulance and ordered the medic to open the back door. I climbed in and explained to the medic about the keys that were in David's pants and that I needed to ride in the ambulance to the hospital. At that very moment David leaned over and reached into his pants pocket and said, "Here let me get you my keys." "Oh no, David, no! Don't move! It is OK, I can ride in here." I immediately tried to get him to lie back down but he already had the keys out. After handing them to me he repositioned himself on the gurney in the ambulance and closed his eyes to rest.

Just minutes before, I was sure my husband had died in my arms and here he was concerned with helping me get into his stinky truck. Seeing him be demonstrative and hearing him talk eased my anxiety some. He was in and out of consciousness but he was alive and aware of his surroundings and that was a good sign, I hoped.

I jumped out of the ambulance, got in his truck and headed out of the parking lot. As I caught up with the ambulance I realized they didn't even have the lights on and they were going the speed limit! *Turn on the sirens! Let's get some emergency service and hurry up! Don't they think this is serious?!* My anxiety began racing again. I picked up my cell to call someone and stared at the phone and felt lost. The only person I wanted to call and tell what was going on and mainly to just ask what to do – was David. The moment was surreal. David is my best friend. He is my first call and my last.

I decided to call my mom but she didn't answer and I left her a message. I didn't make any other calls.

In just under forty-five minutes from the onset of the seizure at Dr. Kelley's office I arrived at the St. John Hospital parking lot and headed towards the emergency room. David had already been admitted when I arrived and by the time I walked into his room they had already begun running a battery of tests on him. I sat next to my husband caressing him and his eyes were shut and not aware of his surroundings.

His diagnosis still inconclusive, they ran more and more tests. They ran more than ten tests in a matter of minutes. Having been to the ER before (one trip earlier that year when Ethan needed stitches from a bicycle tumble and we waited two hours before even getting to fill out the in-take form) I knew from the urgency, something was severe. I called my mom again, no answer.

The looks and stares between the nurses and doctors said more than words. As the nurse looked at a report on the monitor above David's head, she met eyes with the doctor and then they headed out of the room. Something was wrong. I prayed for David and I prayed for God to give me strength.

The results came back from the CT-scan and the doctor came back into the room and only said, "We need to take him for a procedure." After all these tests, glares, rushed actions and they weren't even going to tell me what was going on? David lay on the table, unable to speak, open his eyes or move his body. I asked the doctor adamantly, "Please tell me what has happened!"

The doctor's eyes were sullen; he didn't look directly at me and seemed apologetic telling me these words, his empty words without hope. "Your husband has had a brain aneurysm." The words shot right to my heart and immediately my thoughts went to a friend of Brecka's, Jason, who died in his sleep at thirty years old from a brain aneurysm. I heard his story one afternoon a few years earlier at lunch with Brecka at Jason's restaurant in Catoosa. His story was fresh on my memory as if Brecka had called me earlier in the morning to tell me about it. Jason died of a brain aneurysm. David was going to die. There it was, my biggest fear, Death, and how ironical – it wasn't waiting for me, but for the husband I love.

The doctor hadn't offered any additional information and I needed to know more but I knew we shouldn't be discussing David's condition in his presence, especially if the prognosis was not good. "Can I talk to you in the hall?"

I followed the doctor out to the hallway. He said he wanted to run more tests. I asked, "What does all of this mean?"

"He has had a bleed in his brain and we need to perform a procedure to see if we can stop the bleeding."

"Is this serious?" I asked.

He looked at me with despair and said, "I would call family." And then he rushed off to set up the tests, leaving me standing alone in the stark ER hallway.

All my breath left my body. My knees became weak and I thought I might fall to the floor. Tears spilled down my cheeks before I even realized I was crying. My life just fell out from under me. Jason's death came back to my thoughts. I might only have hours left with my husband.

I walked down the hallway of the ER waiting area. It took an eternity to reach the double doors that led to the waiting room. The waiting area was filled to capacity and as I walked through the crowd, more tears welled up in my eyes. My fear and grief was evident to those watching me pass by.

I called David's sister, Cynthia, as I felt it was most important that his family knew of the news as soon as possible. Cynthia answered the phone cheerfully knowing it was me from her caller ID, "Hello, Adrienne!" I said as clearly as I could through my tears and sobbing, "Cynthia, please just listen to me as I can't speak and as soon as I tell you this news I will have to hang up the phone." I took a deep breath and continued, "David has had an aneurysm and the doctor said that I should contact his family. I think you should come. I don't know anything else and I will call later."

The minute I hung up the phone with Cynthia my phone rang. It was finally my mom. "Mom, David had an aneurysm. We are at St. John. Oh, Mom, I don't know what I am going to do." I hardly made sense through my crying and panic. As I talked, I walked towards the parking garage and towards David's car so that I could "lose it" in private. We exchanged a few words and my mom could tell I *was* losing it. "Adrienne, you have to be strong. Get back in the room with your husband and be strong. I am in Grove and I can be there in an hour."

Instead of immediately going back to the ER, I headed to the truck. I needed a moment alone. A part of me just wanted to hide from reality. I climbed inside, leaned my head on the steering wheel and continued crying, my body now trembling with fear and panic. The worst thoughts raced through my mind. *David is only 40 years old – how could this happen? How could I become a widow at the age of 35? Where would I bury David? Why on Earth did we have that conversation about one of us dying just the night before? How could I go on without David?*

With my head slumped over the steering wheel, I continued to wrestle with feelings of misery and doubt when a message interrupted my depressed thoughts. **Everything is going to be OK.** I hastily ignored the whispered thought and sunk back into despair. *I can't go on alone. I can't replace David.*

Interrupting my thoughts again, the voice flowed

79

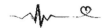

through me again. But that time with more intensity. **EVERYTHING IS GOING TO BE OK.** The voice was so powerful that I instinctively lifted my head from the steering wheel and glanced to the passenger seat as if it came from someone in the truck, just along for the ride. (If only I could have seen right then that He was along for the ride!) As soon as I heard these words, I discounted them. I didn't want to hear the premonition. I didn't want to believe and then be let down. How could I have that kind of blind faith? What if those words were just my subconscious? What if I believed those words and held onto those thoughts and then David died? I ignored the message, put my head back down and cried.

Too much time had passed and I knew I needed to get back to David – I couldn't continue to hide from the reality of what was going on around me. I walked towards the ER and wiped the tears away before entering his room. I entered his room to find him unconscious, with monitors beeping above his head.

I sat next to him and began to argue with God. In my anger I outlined why it shouldn't be David. *Why us God? We have an wonderful relationship. He is my best friend. Why couldn't this be someone that has a terrible relationship? Why us, God, and not someone else?* I was so angry; my self-pity moment quickly started taking over my entire mind and body. I had even lost focus on David. I was focused on being a victim. *Why David...why us?*

And then for the second time a divine message came crashing into my frantic thoughts.

This isn't about ANY of them. This isn't about anyone but David and you. You need to start praying. Pray Adrienne, Pray.

That time I knew it wasn't just a little thought in my head. The message was forceful, specific and direct. A wake up call, you could say! The self-pity left my head and my heart at that moment. I heard God speak to me but that time he commanded me, a commandment that changed my heart, head and path for the days to come. God ordered me to pray and I began to do just that.

CHAPTER EIGHT

CALLING ALL
PRAYER WARRIORS

Opportunity may come through unusual circumstances. Keep your mind open to see.

From the emergency room they took David down the hall to the special procedures area and a nurse led me to a smaller waiting room. The nurse explained that the doctors were going to perform a coiling procedure on David to see if they could stop the bleeding and she asked me to take a seat in the special procedures waiting room.

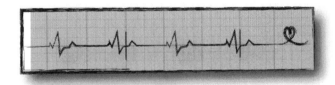

At that point it was four hours into the day and I was very alone and lost in my emotions. I knew I needed to pray but the thoughts from in the stinky truck started racing back through my head. The awareness that Jason died of an aneurysm. I thought David could be in the other room dying. What would I do without him? Our three young children would grow up without knowing their father. How would I take care of our life without him? What would I say at his funeral? I started imaging his funeral. Thinking about our life together and what I would say about David – it was almost as if I was composing his eulogy. My thoughts were racing so fast that I was going through years of memories in seconds. I mentally walked through our life together. Memories from when we met, to the laughter we had shared that morning on the way to the doctor. I thought to myself what a full life we have had. We had been so blessed. I thought, *if this was the end of us, I needed a perfect way to let those at the funeral understand how much he meant to me and how full our life was.* I started scripting out the eulogy in my head.

"David was my everything. Even though David and I only spent 13 years together, our time together was more than some couples experience in a lifetime. David is my Best Friend and he will always be with me." I started to analyze my words, correcting the presentation of delivery and wondering how on Earth I would deliver a eulogy without crying.

My phone rang, thankfully, to save me from my dark thoughts. It was my mother wondering if there had been an update. "I don't know what is going on… They took him in…I will see you in a while."

The special procedures waiting room was about 6' x 6' with no windows and chairs packed in so tight you nearly bumped knees with the person sitting across from you. It obviously wasn't a room designed for extended hanging out time. I was sharing the room with another family. I kept my head down to keep from making eye contact. The last thing I wanted to do at that moment was have small talk with strangers! I wasn't interested with their loved ones' malady but overheard a brief part of the conversation with the nurse as they stepped in the hallway, "Last time your grandmother had this procedure completed it really looked good. We are hoping for a great outcome this time too." I thought, *Grandmother!? I am too young to be in here. What is going on?*

As the time ticked by, I could feel them glancing at me and knew they were curious about my circumstance. I am sure they wanted to know what I was doing in there, all by myself.

I bowed my head and started to pray. *God, Please be with the doctor's hands as they work on David. God, Give me strength to make it through this. Give me strength.*

Then as quickly as my prayer ended, my thoughts started shifting dark again. I started thinking about where I would bury David if he didn't make it through. *It was important that he be buried next to his father in Nebraska; David would roll over in his grave if I put him in Oklahoma soil. As a diehard Husker fan, I could never do that to him.*

I had to get out of that room. The walls began to feel as if they were closing in around me. I was suffocating in that waiting room and I knew if I sat there any longer I would be forced into an insipid conversation about the weather with grandmother's family.

I went to the spacious atrium at the hospital's lobby main waiting area and found a private seat as I surveyed the lobby for any of my family members who may have made their way to the hospital. As I sat there, a scripture came to mind that I had learned five years earlier in Moms on Monday:

> (James 5:14) Is anyone among you sick? Let him call for the elders of the church, and let them pray over him, anointing him with oil in the name of the Lord.

I have never been able to quote scripture and knew

85

that recalling that scripture was a message that I not only needed to continue my prayers but I needed to get busy finding more people to pray for David. I immediately thought of contacting Jim Miller, the pastor of our church, but since his cell number isn't on my contact list, I didn't know how to get in touch with him. I knew the best link was through God. I put my head down in prayer. *God, I need more people praying for David. God, Help me get in touch with Jim Miller. I need to get in touch with him. We need more people praying for David. We need an army of prayer worriers.* After I called for Jim through prayer, I lifted my head up and looked out the glass window. Directly before me was God's answer to my prayer: Henry Haskell, standing at the front entrance of St. John. I shook my head almost in disbelief. I couldn't believe an answer to my prayers would come that quickly.

Henry is a physician at St. John and also a friend of David's and mine from our church Bible study. I don't think that Henry necessarily had Jim's cell phone number on his contact list but I knew he definitely was closer to getting in touch with Jim and the church than I was at the moment. I also knew that I had to be sensitive about getting the information out on one of the many social media outlets that could have thousands of people I didn't know praying for David within minutes. I knew I had to be sensitive for our business and I knew Henry was someone who could handle it confidentially.

I walked outside front toward Henry who was just leaving the hospital and said, "Hi, Henry." A proper Southern gentlemen who is often found wearing his Sunday best seersucker suit, Henry speaks in a slow, calculated voice and uses language that makes you want a dictionary just to keep up with his vocabulary. But that day I almost didn't recognize him in his blue jeans and short sleeve polo. Not typical doctor material.

"Well, Hi, Adrienne. How are you?"

"Not so good. David has had a brain aneurysm."

"Oh. Well, that is too bad," he stated in his typical literalness.

"Henry, I really need your help. I need you to get in touch with Jim and get people at the church praying for David."

"Well, I don't have my cell phone." Henry is Mensa-level smart and his amazing intellect sometimes doesn't translate into the typical entrepreneurial "let's get it done" attitude I was looking for in that crisis situation so I immediately became frustrated at his comment. With a situation as serious as this, I would think anyone would offer immediate assistance so I quickly reacted, "Henry, if you can't do it then never mind."

He could feel my frustration and quickly changed his response, "I am getting picked up right now for lunch and I will use my friend's cell phone."

God put a messenger in my life; Henry was there when I asked God to help. It was obvious that Henry took a while to see he was a messenger but he delivered exactly as intended because within a matter of hours from our encounter in the St. John entrance, not only Jim Miller was praying for David but the entire congregation of First Presbyterian Church.

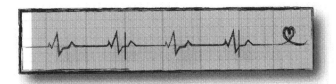

I walked back into the hospital and peeked into the Special Procedures waiting room. There were no nurses, front desk or any way to see David and I needed to stay close in the event that news was delivered of David's condition.

Before that day, I could barely spell the word aneurysm let alone know anything about coiling or understand what was going on in David's head – I wanted to know what they were doing to him. I grabbed my smartphone and started researching "coiling", "aneurysm" and any other information I could find on what was going on.

Aneurysm: A brain (cerebral) aneurysm is a bulging, weak area in the wall of an artery that supplies blood to the brain. In most cases, a brain aneurysm causes no symptoms and goes unnoticed. In rare cases, the brain aneurysm ruptures, releasing blood into the skull and causing a stroke. Symptoms of a ruptured brain aneurysm often come on suddenly. If you have any of the following symptoms or notice them in someone you know, call 911 or other emergency services right away:

- A sudden, severe headache that is different from past headaches.
- Neck pain.
- Nausea and vomiting.
- Sensitivity to light.
- Fainting or loss of consciousness.
- Seizures.

OK, Really? We had all of those! I thought as I continued to read.

Coiling: A catheter inserted into the leg and up into the brain and through platinum coils inserted into the aneurysm, blockage of the blood flow into the aneurysm could be possible.

My research was interrupted as my phone rang. It was my mom checking in to let me know she was close and would be there soon. I headed out to the main lobby to wait for her and I immediately saw my brother-in-law, Kenny. His back was to me and I was close enough that I could hear him on his cell phone, "I haven't been able to find her."

"Kenny" I called from behind. As soon as he turned his face towards me, I began to cry. He was the first family I had seen since the day had begun and the comfort of family was overwhelming. Kenny hugged me and also began to cry. Neither of us knew the outcome and our fears and worries were pouring down our faces.

He asked me questions about David but I didn't have any answers. I told him what had happened over the course of the morning. Even describing the events out loud didn't make it seem any more real.

I had only been talking to Kenny for a few moments when my mom walked into the hospital lobby. She walked up from behind and grabbed my shoulders to turn me around and hug me. As soon as I realized it was my mom, I collapsed in her arms and began sobbing. A mom knows. And my mom more than anyone knows how to get right to where you need support the most. At that moment, I only needed a hug.

We calmed and dried our eyes. "We need to get back to the waiting room because they don't have a way to get in touch with me if he comes out of surgery." I led them back to the special procedures waiting cube. By that time the family I shared the room with earlier had moved on.

We had the room to ourselves and talked openly. They already knew of the morning's events, I began with more details describing what I had learned about an aneurysm. I shared the facts that I pulled off the Internet when the nurse came in to give a post-surgery update. The information she was describing came at me so quickly I couldn't wrap my mind around it. Something about coiling….didn't work….lots of bleeding….trying to find a doctor….has been moved to the 6th floor. I asked her to repeat everything slowly so I could type it into my phone, "Aneurysm. Subarachnoid hemorrhage. Coiling procedure." I understood the main gist: That the procedure was complete, it didn't work, and they had moved him to a room on the 6th floor.

CHAPTER NINE

AN IMPORTANT
APPOINTMENT IN ST. LOUIS

Don't look at a roadblock as a failed opportunity, use a different perspective and find the new path to success.

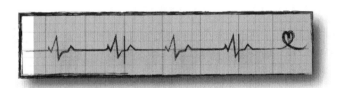

    I wasn't immediately allowed into David's room. We waited in the lobby of the 6th floor, which quickly became family and friend central. As we waited, I continued to search on my smartphone for statistics on David's condition. They were daunting. "A brain aneurysm with subarachnoid hemorrhage has a 50/50 survival rate at the time of rupture. The chances of death following the rupture are still at a 50/50 rate. Those that do survive typically need extended therapy or suffer a lifetime of paralysis. There is a small chance that those with this condition survive and with

a full recovery."

My mom, sitting by my side, interrupted my research when she could tell I was becoming more and more fearful. "Adrienne, you have to put that away, it is only going to get you upset." She was right, I wanted to know everything, but how would my research help me in any way other than getting more worried and upset?

The nurse came to the waiting room to let me know I could go back and see David and that two of us could go in at a time. I asked my mom to come in with me.

He was hooked up to several different monitors. His eyes were closed and he wasn't alert. I immediately walked over to him and wrapped my arms around him. His body was alive, but I had no idea of his mental or physical condition.

The nurses told me they had him on quite a bit of medicine to keep the pain down. She explained that in the coiling procedure, the coils are sent up through the leg and inserted into the bulges in the vein (the aneurysm) in attempts to stop the injury. They showed me the wound at his hip and explained how important it was not to move the area. "He could have life-threatening bleeding so if you see him try to move, contact us immediately." The nurses were matter-of-fact and seemed without compassion as they described David's situation. To them it was the end of a shift, another day, another patient. To me, it was my life that they appeared so spiritless about.

I sat by his side and held his hand, bowed my head and continued my prayers. I started to miss him, even though he was right here. I wanted so badly to talk to him and tell him what was going on.

Friends and family rotated in and out of the room. I called David's sister Carol who was with the kids at home, and told her it was time for her to get up to the hospital. I also decided that it wasn't a good idea to have the children come to the hospital. I hated thinking these thoughts, but knew if Daddy didn't make it through the day or through surgery, I wanted them to remember his sweet goodbye at the house and not the commotion and sadness of everyone at the hospital. Carol headed to the hospital and told me she would find someone to watch the kids.

Dr. Warren Muller from church came to visit David. As he sat next to the bed I asked him if he would pray for David. Dr. Muller said a prayer, I can't even remember if it was silently or out loud. As we finished praying David opened his eyes, looked up at Dr. Muller, and smiled. He didn't say anything, laid his head back down and rested again.

Nurses or on-floor doctors came in at regular intervals to check his vitals and would loudly bark questions. "DAVID CAN YOU MOVE YOUR FEET?" He would feebly push his feet against the nurses' or doctors' hands. "DAVID, CAN YOU RAISE YOUR HANDS?" He would slowly raise his hands. Sometimes it would take the doctor a while to get him to obey the commands. He didn't open his eyes much all day but had been responsive and able to move whatever part of his body they were asking him to move. I knew that must be a good sign, that he was able to understand the commands and move his arms and legs as they asked.

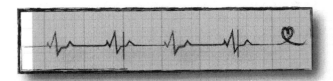

The doctor who performed David's coiling procedure finally made it into his room to talk with me. First he explained in great detail what had happened, repeating some details provided by the nurse at special procedures. I listened intently while my mom stood by. He went on to explain that additional surgery must be performed or his condition could worsen. *Alright, let's operate!* I began to

think.

He then told me the only doctor located in Tulsa who can perform the surgery was on vacation. The closest hospitals are Oklahoma City and St. Louis. He said they had contacted both hospitals and they were trying to get a bed for David. He said they would prefer St. Louis as the hospital there is recognized as a leader in the field of brain injuries.

I stood on one side of David, the doctor the other, his body in a comatose state lying between us. I understood at that moment the life-altering decisions for my husband were in my control.

I also felt right then that he was supposed to be in St. Louis. I don't know why, as one would think my first reaction would be of anger: That time would be against us. That the transportation would be too hard or being away from family or support would be challenging. But nothing I felt was like that. I didn't know anything about the hospital in St. Louis, I just knew that David was supposed to go to St. Louis.

As I came out to tell family and friends that David was being sent to St. Louis for his operation, a friend from church, Amy, was in the waiting room. Amy and I had met through the Moms on Monday Bible study and we had kept in touch off and on over the years. Although not a close friend, the experiences we shared through the Bible study bonded us together in our faith.

She held my hand and asked me a few questions about all that had happened. And then she looked at me in the eyes and said sternly, "Adrienne, I just know he is going to be OK." I immediately started crying when she said these words, remembering hearing the same in David's stinky truck. I still was too scared to believe. Amy also told me to set up an online journal on CaringBridge.com to keep everyone updated on his progress. She said the site was private and she offered help creating the journal if I needed.

My phone had been ringing incessantly all day long.

I typically grab my phone at any time of the day, but today, right then, I couldn't talk to anyone. It was too exhausting. If I didn't have someone on my email or text list, they didn't know what was going on. And everyone knew how important it was for me not to post anything about David's condition on social media outlets. CaringBridge sounded like a great way to get in touch with everyone.

I also began to think about how I was going to tell our franchisees what had happened to David and about how they were going to take the news. I called the office and made preparations for being out of town. A pile of checks was delivered to the hospital for me to sign, appointments were rescheduled and tasks were delegated during my time away from the office.

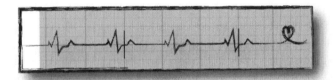

The process of getting David to St. Louis involved planning, insurance and more prayers. The hospital in St. Louis was the Barnes Jewish hospital and the Tulsa medical team worked hard on the phone with their medical team to make sure all the medical codes were approved with insurance so his treatment would be covered at the hospital. The medical codes were provided to the Leer jet ambulance service that was scheduled to fly David to St. Louis. The medical codes were cleared by the hospital in St. Louis so a bed would be held for him. David was a code. He wasn't a person. He was insurance and a code.

I sat in the nurses' station with David's doctors during call after call to the medical air transport and St. Louis hospital. I was anxious about time, as I knew from my earlier online research that every minute David wasn't operated on was another minute his condition could be worsening. I wanted to continue researching about "complications of time delay in operation after a brain aneurysm" but vowed to stop looking at the "what ifs" and just focus on getting through the red tape and help moving his care forward. Once we got approval for the transportation we found out they couldn't charter the plane until a bed opened in St. Louis. There was no bed for David so he had to wait in Tulsa. A life was at risk and we were waiting for a bed!

It was about 7:00 p.m. when my older brother Cameron showed up at the hospital. It was only the second time David opened his eyes during that long day – when he heard Cameron's voice. David looked up and very faintly said, "Hey Cam, what are you doing here?" Knowing that Cameron lives seven hours away in Austin, David appeared surprised, not confused, as to why Cameron was there in his room. We realized then that David had no idea of the seriousness of his situation and we weren't about to let him in on the secret. Cameron had driven in as soon as he heard the news to give him a hug, and be there for me. David rested again and I visited with Cam in the hallway.

My dad, who had arrived a few hours earlier and had kicked into his typical "figure it out" way of operating, was in the nurses' station helping mediate with the hospital staff and insurance company in attempts to push the medical approval process forward and get David to St. Louis. As Cameron and I were standing outside David's room visiting, dad shouted from behind the nurses' station, "We did it! A bed is open!"

We cheered and hugged and the medical air flight team was contacted. But our celebration was quickly defused as we learned that EMT flight crew now had to start their insurance processing before a plane was booked. They couldn't start their process until that bed was booked. I imagined David's bed in St. Louis with his name badge above the headboard. "Welcome David Kallweit!" (Nothing even near this friendly when we did finally arrive.)

Back to the codes, calls and fighting with insurance. Almost two hours later, the EMT flight crew finally arrived.

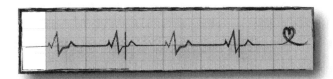

As the EMT flight crew entered the 6th floor of the St. John Hospital it felt like the A-Team had arrived to save the day. They rounded the corner at the nurses' station and it seemed as if time stood still with only Lisa and John, outfitted in green flight gear and med pack gear in arm, moved in slow motion directly towards me. Their confidence exuded as they introduced themselves and said, "We are here to move David to St. Louis." Heroes coming to rescue David!

I had asked my mom to fly with me and my dad decided to drive with my sister Merritt to St. Louis. Even though my mom and I are the *flying scaredy-cats*, we couldn't turn away from David as they transported him to St. Louis. The arrangements were made to get him down to the ambulance and off to the airport and we were escorted in one of the EMT's cars. As my mom and I followed the ambulance, my phone rang. "Hello."

It was Canaan, "Mom, we are scared. The babysitter left us alone at Aunt Carol's." My thoughts instantly went to Carol's apartment that is on the tenth floor of a high-rise condo in Tulsa. Even when I am there only inches away from their side, I fear them slipping over the rail-less balcony edge. To know that they were alone and realizing their freedom to roam without grownups I thought, *They are going to fall to the ground or catch the place on fire!* I went immediately berserk inside my head.

"Where is Carol, Canaan?" I said as calmly as

possible not to reveal that I was scared too!

"The babysitter went to walk the dog and left us here." In all the chaos I hadn't even asked Carol (who had been at the hospital earlier) who she had watching the kids.

"Who is the babysitter? And where is she now?"

"Courtney. Walking the dogs." Courtney was Carol's dog walker. I could feel the blood rushing through my body. My whole life crumbling around me. My husband dying in the ambulance in front of me, my kids stranded on the tenth floor.

I told Canaan to stay on the phone and keep talking to me. Better yet, I wanted all three kids talking to me at the same time. I handed the phone to my mom so she could keep them talking and I took my mom's phone and called Carol. As soon as she answered the phone I started screaming, "WHERE ARE YOU?!! THE KIDS ARE AT YOUR CONDO AND JUST CALLED ME BECAUSE THEY ARE SCARED BECAUSE THEY ARE ALONE. WHY ARE THEY ALONE IN YOUR……" Carol cut me off screaming back, "THEY ARE WITH COURTNEY AND THEY ARE FINE." I yelled, "THEY ARE ALONE AND THE LADY WATCHING THEM LEFT THEM TO GO WALK THE DOGS." Carol tried to reassure me that the kids were fine, that she was just around the corner and that she would call me when she arrived at her house. She then aborted the conversation with a firm, "Goodbye."

The stress of the day that had been building up for us all, had begun to release like a volcano blowing its top. Carol had done everything for David and our family that day, changed her entire schedule so she could arrive at our house early in the morning, stayed with my kids all day keeping them calm, arranging for backup child care so she could get to the hospital and say goodbye to David and even brought my clothes to the hospital so I had something to change into when arriving in St. Louis. She helped David and me selflessly all day long and surely she was insulted for how I treated her, screamed at her. I don't blame her for hanging up on me but to me, my life was falling apart around me and to top it off, a new threat came to the lives of my children as they stayed alone at the high-rise. David was in front of me in a life-threatening situation, getting ready to fly by Leer jet to St. Louis for emergency surgery and my kids were calling on the phone saying they were scared for their life.

I took back the phone that my mom had been talking on with the kids and asked them to keep talking to me. A couple of minutes went by but I could hear all three of them. I could also hear them start picking on each other, which I knew could in fact become more dangerous than the rail-less balcony. I was trying to get their attention to make sure they stayed near the phone when I heard Carol come in the house. I asked Canaan if Carol was there and he said yes. Gratefully, I hung up the phone right as we arrived at the airport. My kids were safe at that point and I knew that the scenario of Carol and me in combat on the phone was not something to which my children should be exposed.

The poor EMT driver witnessed the entire episode. My foul language. My screaming. My insanity. Neither my mom nor I spoke of the matter as we got out of the ambulance and faced the imminent task of getting David onto the plane.

We arrived at the runway at Tulsa International Airport and the EMTs extracted David out of the ambulance. He was on so much pain medicine that he was completely lifeless. Accomplishing the task of loading 225 pounds of comatose David onto a Leer jet with a door the size of a dollhouse entrance was going to be a verifiable act of God.

None of the professionals really had a plan, but they were determined to devise a way to get him onto the plane. The EMT crew and the ambulance crew surrounded David as he lay on the gurney on the runway in the middle of the night. A surreal moment to say the least. They asked my mom and me to get into the plane as far back toward the tail as possible to allow enough room for the seven men and one woman to load David. He took up all of the starboard side of the fuselage! My mom and I scrunched ourselves into our two-seat (seats so small and shaped like triangles) row that barely fit into the rear point of the plane. Strangely enough, it was not at all claustrophobic being in the tail of the Leer jet; the flight space was like a cocooning hidey-hole. It was comforting to me, that after they loaded David into the plane, his feet were practically in my lap so that my mom and I could be close to him and stroke his feet. It was a surreal flight, a clear and beautiful October evening, with stars as bright as diamonds and glittering cities and traffic below us – a moment in time and space like never before or since, to feel the presence of God.

I spent some of my time in prayer during that flight and I have to be honest, that prayer was specifically for me. My fear of flying is ridiculous. Even with David in a life-threatening situation I couldn't relieve my anxiety of flying. I pray before every flight and I did the same then. But that trip I had my mom to lean on and we found laughter in our weakness, making faces and laughing about how scared we were, flying in that dart-like plane. It was good to laugh for the first time all day. Then half way through the flight David started moving and then he mumbled to the EMT sitting next to him, "Where are we?"

The EMT explained to David who he was and where we were and where we were going. They replied simply, offering what he knew and explaining how we were transporting him by Leer jet to St. Louis.

David said softly and in weakness, but you could still understand him and sense his humor, "Great way to travel."

He was the one holding onto the day for *us*! It was an amazing experience to witness David's great inner faith and his never-ending wit and sense of humor! He was a shining light on his own life-saving flight!

Experiencing LOVE

CHAPTER TEN

THE MIDNIGHT ARRIVAL

Don't forget how important rest is for your body. You can tackle anything on a good night's sleep.

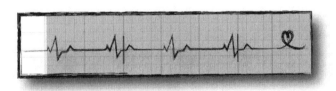

When we arrived in St. Louis an ambulance was waiting at the airport to transport us to the St. Louis Barnes Jewish Hospital. But first we had to get David off of the jet. There were only the two EMTs from the plane and the two EMTs from the ambulance (the two pilots weren't allowed to get involved with loading and unloading of the patient). They began the plan of getting him out of the plane. The female EMT went towards the end of the gurney and the male was outside the plane on the runway holding the front of the gurney. The two of them began maneuvering David

out of the plane when something terrible went wrong. David began bending in half, his head towards his feet. Right then I looked at the gurney and saw it hadn't been locked in place and was folding in half. Both EMTs were struggling and screaming instructions at each other, "He is slipping!"

I immediately reached up and grabbed the end of the gurney that by that time was halfway out of the plane. I pulled on the end and managed to bring David's lifeless body and the gurney back onto the plane in one sweeping motion. Adrenalin was powering all the strength inside of me and if I hadn't grabbed David he would have slid down the gurney and out of the plane to the tarmac below like a toboggan ride.

The EMTs then reloaded David, locked the gurney, and began again to remove him from the plane, watchful of every move. Once into the ambulance, we thanked the EMTs for their help and wished them safety as they flew back to Tulsa. They asked us to keep them updated on David's outcome and gave me their card to keep in touch.

The ambulance ride to the hospital was unbearable. We had never ridden in an ambulance before that moment. Imagine being trapped in a metal box enclosed with medical equipment hanging from above and going through a tornado with no way of holding yourself to your seat. During the ride I first tried to put my hands on David, to be near him but soon realized I needed to put my hands on the side of the ambulance and hold on for dear life. I don't know how David stayed on the stretcher during that ride but they managed to make it to the hospital without throwing him off of the thing.

At the hospital, David was brought in through the back entrance, a series of underground tunnels leading to different wings of the main hospital. The passageways were empty and well lit – very eerie for a middle of the night maze expedition and we definitely didn't want to get lost down there. We ran behind the attendants to keep up with their hurried delivery of David to the 11th floor. He slept through the entire race.

Once on the 11th floor, the attendants set him in the hallway and walked towards the nurse station. "Hey, isn't he going into surgery?" The hospital attendant halfway snickered as he turned around and said, "We have to get him into a room first. His room isn't ready." His bed not only didn't have "Welcome David Kallweit!" above the headboard, but the make-shift hospital room was formerly a medical storage area emptied to accomodate two additional patients due to hospital overcrowding. The nurses told me that my mom and I needed to keep out of the way while they got him situated. We reluctantly left David on the gurney in the hallway and made our way to the waiting room.

In the waiting room we found David's family. Four of his siblings were in the waiting room along with his mother. I had forgotten they would be in St. Louis when we arrived. With all the commotion in Tulsa and fury getting David to St. Louis I had overlooked that other wheels were in motion to get family moved across the nation to be by David's side during that serious time. Calling them seemed like three days ago, not only twelve hours ago.

In those twelve hours his family climbed mountains to get to their brother and son. His brother Keith got a flight from San Francisco leaving immediately from work, with only the clothes on his back, racing down the runway to catch the last plane of the day, he the last passenger boarding. David's sister, Cynthia, brother Steven and his mother left Nebraska at the moment I notified them and drove eight hours together. Janice, the baby of the sisters, took a direct flight from Colorado as soon as she heard the news.

Only two of David's siblings, Carol and Bonnie, were not present. Carol back in Oklahoma caring for our kids and Bonnie, watching from heaven above.

David's family, with whom I feel a closeness as much as with my own, greeted my mom and me with hugs and questions and sympathy. My mom and I approached the room with an energy that didn't reflect the sadness we left behind in Tulsa. Our transportation, flight and ambulance ride, got our mind out of the sadness for a moment. But once we arrived we were reminded of the fierce situation we were facing. David's family had been sitting in St. Louis with only the unknown to wrestle with, without the ability of seeing David, and their pain and confusion was reflected in their eyes. I wanted first to find a way to get David's family in to see him and soon I found a doctor who could help us get into his room.

David's admitting doctor, who couldn't have been older than 25 years, came in to talk with us about what was going on with David, ask us questions, and provide answers to some of our questions. He went over David's condition, which he explained in detail, mainly for David's family who hadn't been with us in the Tulsa hospital. He started with the basics that likely are told to all patients' families upon arrival at Barnes Jewish, first describing to the family a basic definition of the aneurysm and then explaining more about why they rupture. He went on with more general information, "The subarachnoid hemorrhage occurs when a blood vessel on the surface of the brain ruptures and bleeds into the space between the brain and the skull. An aneurysm is a blood-filled pouch that balloons out from an artery wall." Much that he described was general information that I had learned by that point, but his confidence and knowledge was immediately comforting. David's family jotted down notes as they learned about David's condition.

I had so many questions and wanted to first understand why did the rupture occur? *Did I stress him out that morning when I didn't get up with our alarm that I caused his blood vessel to burst?!* "What caused the rupture? Can stress cause it?" He stated that there are no clear reasons why people have a ruptured aneurysm. Stress is not linked as a cause but definitely high blood pressure (hypertension) is the most common cause. The doctor confirmed that they were aware from David's chart he has high blood pressure and is on medication for it.

We all had questions about survival rates and lifestyle following the injury; however, most of the questions we had for the young doctor, he could not answer. Not that he didn't have the information, but I felt he could not be conclusive, positively or negatively, not knowing what the outcome would be. And I definitely could tell there was more that they weren't telling me. In lieu of definitively outlining the outcome, he provided some comfort, "David's neurosurgeon who will be performing surgery later in the day is Dr. Chicoine. Dr. Chicoine is a very skilled doctor and he and his team will take great care of David during surgery."

He then paused and added with a clear and instructive tone, "You must know that things are very serious for David as he has a severe bleed. David does not have a single rupture, which is most common, but he has several tears and we will have to perform surgery to attempt to clip the different ruptures."

From the time we left Tulsa I had begun to feel slightly relieved about David's condition as David was talking some, moving more and even expressing his sense of humor through quiet comments to us on the airplane. But that conversation with the admitting doctor left me confused and filled with anxiety all over again. His words were not hopeful or uplifting but rather fact-filled yet inconclusive. Not even helpful information but rather, stressed the fact that the rupture is much more than a normal aneurysm as his contained multiple tears resulting in a lot of bleeding. He didn't say to us whether or not patients had lived or died after that point, and I knew that he was intentionally leaving a very crucial fact out – the fact that his chances of survival

were still narrowing.

Within the walls of the Tulsa hospital, I had already wrestled with the reality of possibly losing David so I tried to hold strong through the doctor's words; however, the idea of David's promising improvement had been silenced. Especially since I knew here at Barnes Jewish we were dealing with the experts – this hospital admitted patients in David's condition daily.

The doctor then asked us some questions about David's health for his chart. I mainly answered questions about his current medications and his family added in family health information such as a history of heart disease. The only item that the doctor seemed particularly interested in was David's high blood pressure. He asked me what medication David was taking and if he was taking it regularly. I never monitored David's pill-taking so I couldn't answer conclusively whether or not he was taking it regularly. But it was clear there was a concern and that likely could be an important key in the aneurysm rupture.

Before he concluded with us, he said that it would be best if we didn't visit David's room too much through the night as he needed as much rest as possible but we could take short visits, one person at a time.

David's family immediately stood up to go into his room for a visit, having not seen David since the terrible news had been passed through their family. Having just been with David throughout the flight and the ambulance ride, I sat back in the waiting room and let his family go in. I began to process through my mind the conversation we had with the doctor, thinking about what was really going on with my husband. His head gushing with blood, bleeding from multiple tears and his brain cavity filled. I became concerned with his mental state, whether it had already become compromised and what was to come.

Within a short time, the presence of so many Kallweit family members, a struggle grew between the nurses' authority over David's care and our compassion to be near him. A power struggle was battled throughout the early morning hours as we continued to visit David off and on while receiving glares and glances of disapproval from the nurses. David wasn't very coherent and he didn't open his eyes or talk much; however, he continued to respond to the demands from the doctors to test vitals and responses. David's mom was deeply saddened seeing her son in that situation. She stayed by his side much of the night and remained in the room into the morning hours.

My anxiety rose through every passing moment as I knew time was of the essence in saving David. We were told in Tulsa that David would go immediately into surgery the *minute* we arrived at the hospital in St. Louis. This information was greatly contradicted once we arrived in St. Louis and David was plopped in the hallway. We learned there were many steps and procedures that must be completed before David was even in line for surgery.

The stares and grunts continued from the nurses who insinuated that we needed to get out of his room and let David sleep. Since it was around 3:00am and we all were exhausted, everyone acquiesced to the requests and retreated to their reserved rooms in the hotel that is conveniently connected to the hospital.

I couldn't leave David so I attempted to sleep on two chairs pulled together in the middle of the waiting area that was just an arm's reach from his patient room. With all the family gone and surrounded with silence, I could hear the buzz of the soda and snack machines so loud that they kept me from even dozing off for a few moments of sleep. I looked down at my shoes, thinking how gross and dirty they were, and thanking God I didn't wear those heels – those

Experiencing LOVE

shoes *had* covered a lot of ground that day.

I couldn't sleep. I picked up my phone to check emails and voicemails. I again thought of how I hadn't been able to *talk* to David all day. When David and I aren't talking we are texting each other throughout the day and I decided to send him a text:

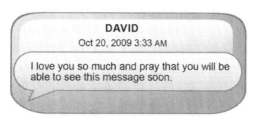

DAVID
Oct 20, 2009 3:33 AM

I love you so much and pray that you will be able to see this message soon.

Wanting to fill these empty moments, I thought it was as good a time as any to send our franchisees an email to inform them what was going on with David. I pulled out my computer to draft an email. I wanted to be as positive in the message as possible. I thought about our franchisees and their families and wanted to stay strong for them and let them know that SeekingSitters would not be affected. I was in charge of everything at that moment, of the business that David and I had built together. I hadn't made a decision before without his approval or guidance and there I was, on my own.

To: All Franchisees	
From: Adrienne Kallweit	
Subject: Important News	October 20, 2009 3:44 AM

Dear Franchisees:

Yesterday morning (Monday) David was taken to the emergency room for a head pain. He has an aneurysm and we are now in St. Louis. He has had very stable vital signs and has been alert all day. He will go into surgery at 6:00am and we will keep you updated when we know more. Please keep David in your prayers.

Please know that we have taken measures to make sure the franchise system is managed as efficiently as always and have plans in place as we move forward. We have an amazing team that has handled the office with ease when we have been out of town on numerous occasions and I have complete confidence in them that they can help you with any of your needs while I am with David. Please direct all your questions or concerns to the team at the office.

Adrienne Kallweit, President
SeekingSitters Franchise System, Inc.

Experiencing L O V E

112

CHAPTER ELEVEN

IT'S JUST
BRAIN SURGERY

Humor holds so much power. Humor can diffuse an argument, improve health and strengthen relationships. Because of this, look for humor in every part of your life. Or find someone who reminds you to laugh.

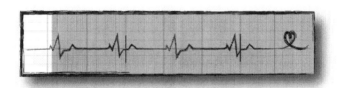

David has a wonderful sense of humor. We have much humor in our marriage and he can always find away to defuse any tense moment with a jocular comment or witty joke. It is his personality but also his way of dealing with

stressful situations. A big part of our family life is our good-natured laughing and teasing and he has reminded me over the years to balance my sometimes serious way of thinking with humor. I wished for his humor at that time – a positive boost during those critical hours awaiting surgery.

We anticipated a 6:00 a.m. surgery time. Our early morning meeting with the admitting doctor revealed many steps must be carried out before David would land on Dr. Chicoine's operating table. The admitting doctor gave us the details of the surgery and what they would do to David. All I could think was, *Really, you are going to cut into his brain?* He gave a step-by-step account of how they were going to perform surgery on David. It all sounded like science fiction. All the family listened to the doctor explain how they would cut a rectangular piece out of his skull and reach their hands into David's brain and place metal clips on the ruptured areas to prevent further bleeding. *Really, cut into his brain and put your fingers in there and he will survive? Is that even possible? Have they performed this before on a human or is David like the guinea pig test study case?* I was entering into some sci-fi movie mystery and wanted the *MythBusters* team to take a whack at what they were going to do to see if it would work first.

The brain surgery was scheduled for around 10:00 a.m., so I thought I would have time to take a shower and change from the disgusting clothes I had been wearing for almost two days, in which I'd even slept on the floor of the hospital waiting area. I had not left David's side since Monday morning and it was hard to step away, but since I hadn't slept in over thirty hours it seemed that a short break to shower would be good.

I walked to the hotel room that my parents stayed in the evening prior and used their shower. I wanted to hurry so I could get back to David but I also wanted to have a moment to breathe. I stood in the shower with the hot water running and dozed off, mind-numbed. I had cried so many tears and hadn't slept in two days and my thoughts were gone. I was simply sad. I stood in the shower for no more than 10 minutes when I thought it would be best to get back to the hospital room.

Just as I was drying off with a wonderfully fresh-smelling hotel towel, my phone rang and it was my mom's number. "David is talking and he is asking for you," my mom said anxiously. "Hurry!"

"Oh, no! Are you serious?! I am on my way." I thought to myself, *Are you kidding me!? I step away for two seconds and now he is awake and asks for me. I attempted to sleep on the floor in a dirty hospital room to be near him and now he is going to think that I haven't been there for him.* I rushed to dry off, threw clothes on and without even drying my hair ran from the hotel room to the hospital and back to the waiting area in surgery prep. As I walked up I could see David's mom, sister Cynthia and my mom all surrounding him. His eyes were closed but I could see him subtly motioning with his hands while he was talking to them.

I walked up to him and laid my head on his chest as he used all his strength to pull his arms around me with the IVs tugging at his arms, yet determined to be as close to me as he could. I could feel his chest gently move up and down as he breathed and just for a brief few seconds the hospital sounds disappeared and it was as if nothing bad had ever happened and we were going ahead with life like always. He said "I love you." It felt so good to hear these words. I began to cry and said "I love you, too."

He raised his head and looked up at me for a brief moment. I saw his eyes, his beautiful green gray eyes, that had been closed for most of the past 24 hours and then he closed his eyes again and continued to hug me.

He then said, "Tell the kids I love them." I asked him if he knew what was going on. He said they just told him he was getting ready to go into surgery. I explained to him that

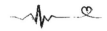

they were operating on his brain and they were going to clamp the ruptures from the aneurysm. He could tell by my solemn tone that I was distressed and said, "I am going to be OK."

We continued to wait by his side in the surgery prep area for several more hours. Anxious with every passing minute, we learned the surgery ahead of us had taken a turn for the worse and was taking longer than expected. The news made us more uneasy. David had fallen back to sleep while everyone gathered close by.

David's family was dealing with the situation much differently than mine – notably with an absence of humor among them. As they surrounded David with sorrowful eyes, stroking his arm and hugging him while he slept. My family reacted quite differently, as with most situations of stress and danger, we react with nervous laughter. In my family we laugh when we should be crying, in serious situations or when something terrible happens. My mom and I sat with David, told funny stories and ate bananas. Yes, bananas in the surgery prep area! Bananas or any food in the surgery prep room is taboo, which I learned when a nurse caught me tossing away the peel.

The time finally arrived. Around 12:30 p.m. we were notified that David was next in line for surgery. One by one the family gave him their "I love yous" and touched him in their own special way.

David opened his eyes for a brief moment, looked up at us and said, "What are you all so worried about? It isn't like I'm having brain surgery." He paused and then said, "Oh wait, I am." And there it was – David's wonderful sense of humor even in a life-and-death moment! His witty comment cut through the solemn atmosphere and I, along with everyone else, could not hold back tears of thankfulness for my wonderful man's spirit and inner strength. David then was wheeled away and he disappeared behind nurses and doctors. But out from underneath the blanket came his arm with his fist in the air - David was giving a triumphant Thumbs Up! My mom and Cynthia cheered with joy and I caught that amazing moment on my phone camera.

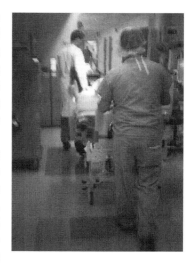

We moved into the ICU waiting area in anticipation of the update calls from the nurse. While the hours passed, I entertained myself by people-watching as there were many other families awaiting surgery outcomes. I particularly noticed a woman that was crying, huddled up in the corner with family hovered around her. She was covered with a large blanket as if she had been there overnight.

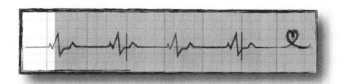

I got the first call from surgery after we had been waiting almost two hours: "Surgery started around 2:00 p.m. and they are making their first incision now and almost have the skull open." I heard the sound of a buzz saw in the background and it was all I could do to maintain my composure – that was *my husband's* head they were sawing on, and the sound was no different than the noise I had so often heard on construction sites! I was dumbfounded and couldn't think of anything much to say or ask after the impact of that news, so I replied in a feeble, almost

117

incoherent voice, "Thank you and I look forward to you calling again." It was strange, like a dream, I was out of my body talking to someone I didn't know, about someone else I didn't know who was having his skull sawed off.

I relayed the message to the family, but spared them the agony of knowing about the sounds in the background. I prayed. *God, Please help the doctors with their steady hand and help them perform every movement with skill and expertise. God, Give me strength.*

I texted everyone I had been communicating with throughout the day and let them know that surgery had begun and to please start praying.

There were reports on David's status every few hours. They called when the clips were successfully implanted in his head. They called again as they were putting his skull back together. Through our wait we learned his was the doctor's third brain surgery that day.

Cynthia expressed the concerns she was having for me, "I am so scared for you. You have your business and your children. I don't know what you are going to do." I assured her that I would figure it out. I said I had to keep praying and I knew I had strength through God for whatever the outcome would be. She and her family helped me through those long hours with lots of hugs and support as we waited for David. I did the same for them.

Meanwhile I went across the room to see the woman that I noticed in the corner earlier. As soon as I walked up to her, she began to talk to me as if we had known each other for years. She told me she was thirty eight years old, had three small children, all just four years older than mine, and her husband had just come out from surgery to remove a brain tumor discovered several months earlier. Dr. Chicoine also operated on her husband – the first of three brain surgeries that he performed that day. The similarities of our situations forged an immediate bond between us. She said the surgery was successful but he lost hearing in his right ear and would never hear again. Earlier in the day she was an absolute wreck, crying and agonizing over fear for her husband's health and her family's welfare and while talking she asked me how I could be so calm under the circumstances. I paused as I reflected on her question – realizing we were in similar situations but handling it much differently. I knew exactly where my strength was coming from, "I have been praying constantly for strength."

She said that one hard part of the experience that she didn't expect was the stress on the family and she warned me to be patient. I didn't understand what she meant at the time but throughout David's hospitalization I would come to know intimately the stress it can cause, especially to family relationships.

I decided to take Amy's advice and set up the account on CaringBridge to let people know about David's progress. That could give me an outlet to be productive, which helps me cope: getting things done – a project. I spent time researching the CaringBridge website, as I needed to be sensitive about the information posted online and I requested for people to remove Facebook posts about David's status. CaringBridge would be a great way to get information to our church congregation as well as our family and friends back home. I set up an account and posted a general story of what had happened to David over the past 36 hours. I decided I would make another post on the site after surgery and put the computer away.

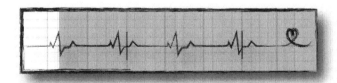

A little over eight hours after surgery begun we got the final call that everything was completed. Even though it had only been 36 hours since David passed out in our

bathroom at home to the point that brain surgery in St. Louis, Missouri had been completed for me, time had no conceptual quality any longer and it seemed like weeks since the accident.

The brain surgeon met with our family to give us David's prognosis. That was the first time I had met his doctor and as we shook hands to introduce ourselves I distinctly remember the feel of his hand in mine – it was cool and steady, and I thought, *These hands were just inside my husband's brain.* But I just said to Dr. Chicoine, "Thank you." It was all I could say. He led our family of eight into a room that was so small it was surprising how all of us fit. But everyone found a space for themselves and listened intently to the brain surgeon's every word, patiently explaining that the surgery was successful. "We cut a rectangular incision out of David's skull and then went in and clipped off the four ruptured areas. This is very extensive, as typically only one clip is applied. David had a very severe rupture. He has a shunt in his skull to drain off the fluids and we will continue to monitor this as well as monitor for vasospasms." Dr. Chicoine explained that the vasospasms were kind of like aftershocks, mini-strokes, that commonly occur following an aneurysm. These can be life-threatening and can cause further neurological damage and the critical period is four to ten days following surgery.

The questioning started with David's sister Cynthia leading the inquisition, asking what his life would be like after surgery and how would he recover from the aneurysm. I was thankful for her attentiveness as I wasn't able to formulate any questions with all the overwhelming information. Dr. Chicoine couldn't offer a lot of definitive answers and it would become clear throughout our stay at Barnes Jewish Hospital that the physician's code of conduct was to be vague and not offer a positive or negative comment about any outcome for liability reasons. "He should be coming out of anesthesia very soon and you can see him" were the doctor's final words.

Soon, I was told I could go back to see David – I took my sister Merritt with me to the 11th floor ICU entrance. It was an intimidating place! Two large reverse-opening double doors led to the ICU patient area that required authorization for entrance. The nurse waived her passkey over the call button and the double doors swung open revealing the long hallway of patient rooms inside. In his wing there were five rooms on the left and five rooms on the right. Each small room was only large enough for a bed, side chair and monitoring equipment. The rooms lacked privacy, with a glass wall and open doorway their only separation from the hallway. Monitors at the many nurses' stations – one nurse station for every two rooms – were beeping with different codes and warnings for each patient room. We could see in some rooms the patients lying in misery and some rooms with the curtains shut for privacy, but every room was full.

David's room was the second on the left and as soon as we entered the hallway we could hear David screaming. As we entered his room we could see the nurses were struggling to secure his arms to his hospital bed with canvas straps. He was trying to get out of the hospital! He was raging with anger and his strength was stronger than the two nurses holding him down. He looked right up at me, eyes wide open and with all his might he shouted to me, "GET ME OUT OF HERE, ADRIENNE. GET MY SOCKS AND SHOES, LET'S GO!" Then he counted down very loudly from 5 to 1 just like we do for our kids when they must mind us immediately: "5….4….3….2….1!"

Merritt and I stood there in astonishment – and began laughing! Yes, nervous laughter, that is our family's stress-coping mechanism – but at that moment David's outburst was so unexpected, so crazy-funny. There he was just one hour out of brain surgery and demanding to get out of the hospital. We exited pronto and left that raging bull

for the nurses! We would come back once he had settled down.

When we returned about an hour later, David was much calmer and they had removed the arm straps but there was no mistaking his discomfort. He was miserable – the anesthesia was wearing off and he was starting to feel the excruciating pain.

A nurse came to give a neurological exam and we saw both his arms raised in the air in response to her commands. She said, "Turn your wrists in," and he turned them in. His right hand flopped to his chest and she said, "No. Put your arm back up," and he did. She said, "Turn your wrist out," and he did. "Hold your arms still," she said. He kept his arms up in the air for a count of five seconds and then she said, "OK. You can put them down now," and he let both arms flop on his belly, after which he proclaimed, "JELLO!"

How can a person whose loved one is balancing on the narrow line between life and death burst out with laughter? But I did! I was elated to know David had not lost his precious soul – in his darkest moment he gave me laughter when it was I who should have been giving him a get-well bouquet of flowers! But his physical description was far from humorous. He had one tube coming out of his head (the "brain drain," we coined it) and tubes in his arms and legs. There were machines that were giving him fluids, taking fluids out of him and monitoring every vital sign he could be tested for. I told him the family would come to see him, which they did, two at a time – doctor's orders. They inspected the tubes coming out of his arms, neck and head and they comforted him while he went in and out of sleep. He was dazed from the medications and weak from surgery but he recognized everyone and was able to speak a few words, mostly complaining about the pain. David's mom took it very hard and sobbed quietly beside him, so fearful for his life. I could feel her agony, the thought of her youngest child dying. She had already lost her oldest child to breast cancer and the thought of losing a second child during her lifetime seemed at the moment just too much to bear. She held and stroked his hand and kissed his head.

I went into the room again with his brother Keith. As Keith stood over him, he started asking David questions to test his memory. Keith asked some general questions, "Where were you born?" "What is my name?" and so on and then said, "What color is Adrienne's hair?" A trick question, as I tend to change my hair color about as much as others change clothes and have been doing so since I discovered my first gray hair in college! To Keith's question, David answered groggily but without hesitation, "Gray." Keith and I laughed at David's humor.

After everyone was able to visit with David we decided that it would be best to leave him alone to rest for the night and for us to rest as well. I thought it would be a good time for me to sleep since I hadn't slept in two days. I walked back with my family to their hotel room and got ready for bed. I asked Merritt if she could make a post on the CaringBridge site before we all went to bed:

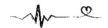
WEDNESDAY, OCTOBER 20, 2009 11:37PM, CDT   CARINGBRIDGE.ORG

This is Merritt, Adrienne's sister. Surgery is completed and everything went as expected and it was a success. However, this is just the first step to recovery. He is in the best care team and best doctors across the nation.

David can move all his body parts and knows who is in the room. He is in pain but the pain is being controlled with heavy pain narcotics. The nurse said that David was doing well, considering. Adrienne is holding up very well. She is a pillar of strength and faith and is there for David and his family.

Thank you for your prayers and please continue to pray as God is definitely performing miracles for David.

Experiencing LOVE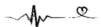

CHAPTER TWELVE

KEEP MOVING FORWARD

I have to be often reminded, I can't control everything.

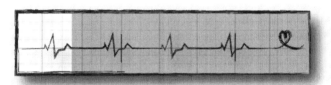

I returned the next morning at about 6:00 a.m., unable to sleep from thinking about David alone in the ICU room and not knowing how his night had gone. I threw on clothes but no makeup and headed towards his room through the corridor that connected the hotel and hospital, a path I would come to know well. As I arrived, the nurses stopped me before I went into his room and said David had a rough night and that he was in quite a bit of pain but he was sleeping now. I asked if they had to strap him down over the night. They said no but reiterated that he was in quite a bit of pain. I asked if I could talk with his doctor but the nurse said he wouldn't be making rounds until around 7:30 a.m. The non-visiting hours between 6:00 a.m. - 8:00 a.m. and 6:00 p.m. - 8:00 p.m. allow the doctors time for rounds without family intrusions; however, the nurse said that if I stayed quiet I could stay in the room so I could talk to the doctor.

As I waited and David slept I learned more about the 11th floor of the Barnes Jewish Hospital from the nurses assigned to David. The 11th floor was an all-brain-patient ICU and Barnes Jewish Hospital is one of the top, if not the top, neuroscience center in the country, with some of the most skilled neurosurgeons in the nation. The 11th floor ICU unit had patients with conditions ranging from brain tumors, brain injuries due to blunt force, brain injuries due to stroke or aneurysm. To the 11th floor nurses, brain injuries were like broken arms to an average hospital emergency room. I remembered how it was when I gave birth to my firstborn, watching through the glass window, observing the neonatal nurses while they whipped the babies around checking vitals, taking measurements, changing diapers and learning from them how I could handle my own newborn, all the while fearing that one wrong move would break him. These 11th floor nurses did the same with the brain patients. They effortlessly maneuvered brain drains, cleaned stitches, changed out IVs, checked charts and administered medications. We were in the best care possible and I thanked God again for His mercy in delivering David to St. Louis.

The display monitoring his temperature would beep every ten minutes or so. The nurse told me they were concerned about his fever, but not overly, as it was normal to have a high temperature to fight off the infection. They would keep an eye on the fever since it was so high.

The doctor arrived around 7:30 a.m. while David was still sleeping. He wasn't his main surgeon, Dr. Chicoine, but the morning floor doctor. He reviewed x-rays of David's brain and explained to me the x-ray on the right was the picture taken in Tulsa when the bleed first happened and you could see the evidences of increased blood in his brain and what was 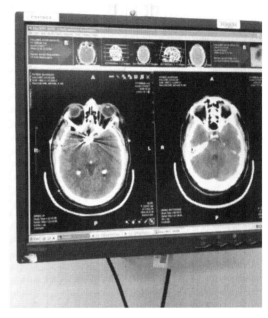 causing the pressure and pain in his head. He said that the blood would eventually naturally be absorbed by his body and showed me, in the pictures on the left (taken immediately following surgery), the metal clips that were now in David's head. The clips were shining in the x-ray like diamonds in the middle of his head.

I asked the doctor many questions of the recovery forecast, again many answers of which could not be provided. He explained that the tube in his head (the brain drain) is regulating the fluids inside his skull. He said that typically David would stay in the ICU until he recovers and the tube is removed. We must watch him closely as the vasospasms could be life threatening. He said most patients are transferred to an assisted living facility following surgery and the hospital stay, to complete their recovery, but there was no sure way of knowing how quickly David would

129

recover, especially with the extent of his injury. He reaffirmed the intensity of the bleed and that David's injury was a very serious condition. I asked a question that haunted me: *Do you know why this happened?* He said there's no known reason for David's particular bleed. I took pictures of the x-rays; David slept through the entire conversation.

David's family arrived at the hospital room around 8:00 a.m. As they made their way I explained what the doctor said and showed them the pictures from the x-ray. It was difficult to find peace and hold on to strength with so many people around so I took some time to walk the hospital and get a break and let David's family be with him.

That first day of recovery was very hard. I was stressed, tired, worn out and terribly sad. I felt like I was the person that needed to be making the decisions for David as his wife and his life now; however, with all the family members there, his and mine both, it was becoming stressful. Everyone wanted to help with decision making and caretaking. There were family members in and out of his room, nurses constantly monitoring and doctors making their visits and David's room seemed like party central.

The doctors and nurses had given us instructions that in the ICU he is only allowed two visitors at a time and it was important that everyone wash their hands so that the patient stays well during the healing period. Trying to hold it together, I did so by attempting to control everything. I kept a strict watch on how many people were coming in his room at a time, sometimes getting pushed out myself to meet the two-per-room demands. I was definitely neurotic about the germs. Much like a new mother forcing everyone who touches her new baby to sterilize their hands with hot soapy water. I was freaked out by anyone who sneezed, coughed, didn't scrub down from head to toe or simply touched David. Looking back, my neurosis was ridiculous but I felt I should control everything in the environment to help make a no-complications recovery for David. And these were the doctor's orders, OK may...be taken a bit to the extreme, but they were the orders. I had even asked David's mom at one point to please wash her hands as she entered the room and she quickly reminded me, "Adrienne, I raised seven children and I was the one who raised David. I think I know what I need to do."

But I did quickly begin to poke fun at myself and my neurotic behavior and snapped a picture of David's sister Janice as I forced her, along with everyone else, to wear masks during that first 24 hours while anyone visited him in the ICU.

David's fever remained high but he started opening his eyes more during the day. For David, the day consisted of lots of rest, and repeated neurological tests from nurses asking the same three questions they would almost yell to every patient throughout the ICU: "WHAT IS YOUR NAME? WHAT DAY IS IT? WHAT HOSPITAL ARE WE IN?"

♡ ♡ ♡

During the evening non-visiting hours, we decided it was a good time to head back to the hotel and get some sleep for the night. When we got to the room my mom could tell I needed to talk and asked if I was OK.

My thoughts were jumbled. *There were so many stresses. No sleep, tight spaces, the unknown, everyone wanting to be in control, everyone in fear.* I revealed the stress that I was feeling, that I felt like I was getting pushed

131

out of the way and being disregarded as David's wife and that my role was being usurped by all the well-meaning relatives. I wished everyone knew what an important part of each other's lives David and I are. There isn't a day that I don't talk to him and even though I was sitting there with him during every moment of his recovery, I wasn't talking with him. I felt like a part of me was missing.

My mom always has a way of finding perspective in every moment. "Adrienne, a traumatic event such as this will bring stress and strain on a family. You have to hold onto the fact that you are David's life and not let the stress of anyone around you affect your purpose right now, which is to be here to protect and cherish David. Our main prayer is that David heals miraculously but do know that whatever may come of David's time here in Barnes Jewish and after he goes home, you will be strong. You will move forward and you can be strong on your own. And your children will be strong. Don't live in the 'what if' and stress of this situation. Remember to look toward the good that tomorrow will bring while you are focusing on the positive outcome of today."

She told me to stand strong for my role as David's wife as I am the most important person in his life, reminding me of the scripture in the bible where husband and wife become one flesh. So I should not feel guilt or anger for being overprotective of David, but respect my family for what they have given me and have patience in the time they were there.

Her words put me completely at peace and I knew in my heart the relationship David and I have and the strength that we have together as one, we would make it through.

Before I went to bed I spent some time updating the world on David's condition through the CaringBridge site:

We spent lots of time with David tonight. I read him all the messages from this site and he loved hearing all the messages from friends and family. He dozes off and I would ask him if he wanted me to keep reading and he would always nod yes. He doesn't talk a lot - not a lot of energy, but can answer questions. He has had his eyes closed most all the time since Monday - but tonight he had his eyes open a lot and even laughed with us...of course he was laughing about jokes regarding the bath the nurse gave him.

Talked to the Dr.'s tonight and he said David is doing well, but we have a long way to go. He is concerned about some things and will be running tests tomorrow. They said that they will be having him walk around tomorrow. His temp has lowered and he is feeling good.

After I finished the message, I tried to go to sleep but my hope for strength morphed into fear. I couldn't stop thinking about David in the ICU by himself. I rolled over and started crying silently to keep from waking my parents in the other bed, as I was sharing the hotel room with them. I talked to God in prayer, thanks the many blessings that we had received throughout the day and also prayed for

strength. But still felt so scared and alone. I had my phone next to me and sent David a text:

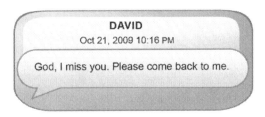

DAVID
Oct 21, 2009 10:16 PM

God, I miss you. Please come back to me.

I slept restlessly and finally decided to get up around 6:30 a.m. I dressed and went straight to David's room. He was asleep but began to wake soon after and started squirming and opened his eyes and looked straight at me and said, as if we had been apart for days (which I guess we had), "I have missed you." I said, "I have missed you, too." He then said groggily, "Please don't leave me again."

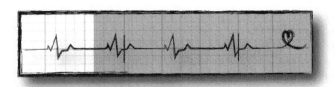

David seemed to be progressing well. He ate breakfast and opened, on his own, two orange juice cups and drank them - which was a huge accomplishment. I could tell he was pushing himself to gain back his strength. He could talk and remember things (but we didn't talk about what had just happened over the course of the past 72 hours.) He said he felt like he had been hit by a Mack truck and constantly asked for more pain medicine. The nurses insisted that they gave him the maximum allowed and he continued to argue that it hadn't kicked in.

I spent most of the day by David's side in prayer. When I'm at home there's so much distracting noise in the house and at the office, but the hospital cacophony of beeps, chimes, hushed voices and patient moans took a background to my meditations. I sat by his bedside and prayed quietly for him. I could feel the presence of other prayers coming through for David. I don't know how to explain it but it was as if when I sat there in prayer I wasn't alone. I would pray and then I could feel others praying for him. I could almost hear and feel the presence of other's prayers. I haven't ever felt this before and haven't felt this feeling since. It was such an overpowering presence that it's almost impossible to describe.

The nurses told me later that afternoon they were planning to get him walking. It was important for him to walk as soon as possible so that blood clots wouldn't form in his legs. By that point I had relaxed a bit about the germs and at least allowed everyone to ditch the masks, but constant washing of hands remained necessary. I was just so fearful still, that I continued to attempt to control everything.

After nearly four days horizontal, it had come time to get David up and walking. They put straps around his legs to help him stand and around his waist to help him up from the bed. It took a while but they did get David up out of his bed and helped him take a few steps across the room into the main entry area of the ICU. By the time he was up and walking the word had spread, and the entire family that was in the waiting room came rushing in the ICU and were all standing around David and cheering for him as if he was crossing a marathon finish line. There were about eight family members watching the momentous occasion. (If you are keeping track as closely as I was – that is six more visitors than allowed!) Everyone was marveling at his accomplishment but my excitement to see him walking quickly turned to anxiousness about his healthy recovery

135

that I wanted to follow the doctors' and nurses' every order. I was so angry at the crowd in the ICU room that I walked out to make room for the other family members that were gathered around David while he made these first momentous steps.

I am very sure my anger came from stress and fear of the unknown. *Will David be in therapy for the next year? What will it be like for our family not to have our strong David around the house taking care of us? Will he regain full use of all his limbs? Will I be taking care of him? Will he be able ever to return to work?* I wanted to scream for everyone to leave. *I will be the one taking care of him for years to come, not you all!*

Even though it was only under 48 hours since surgery was completed, it was evident that David was on his way to recovering (and likely evident my frustrations were brewing) so family, one by one, started to schedule their returns home.

After his first walk, David's sister Janice had to head home to Colorado and said her goodbyes to her brother. David hugged her goodbye. My parents were also planning to leave that afternoon but not before my dad drove 20 miles around St. Louis looking for a Wendy's Frosty per David's request. Once the Frosty was delivered, my mom, dad and sister said their goodbyes.

Following the afternoon goodbyes, the rest of the family went to their hotel rooms for a break. I checked in on the kids who were with their afterschool babysitter then responded to a few work emails. To any outsiders who didn't know about David's aneurysm, it seemed like life as normal. I was tending to everything that I needed to with work and with the help of our office team; nothing was falling through the cracks. A quick email to the office crew:

To:	Christina, Kevin
From:	Adrienne Kallweit
Subject:	Checking In

October 22, 2009 4:35 PM

Hi guys!

Just wanted to check in and see how you all are doing. When I was talking to David this morning I told him all was held down on the office home front and he smiled. My mom and dad are going to be in the office on Friday and through next week so please lean on them if you need anything. They will bring stories from here too. I will be back on Tuesday & Wednesday of next week for training – then back to St. Louis until he gets to come home to Tulsa. All is looking good so far. The critical recovery days are 4-10 and day 4 is tomorrow. David was up and walking today and I am attaching a picture that is NOT to be passed out, please ☺ I will leave it up to David if he ever lets anyone see the pictures outside of you guys – but just wanted you all to get to see him smiling!

After finishing the message I attached the least revealing picture of that first walk through the ICU and hit send.

I received a response back while I was still online working.

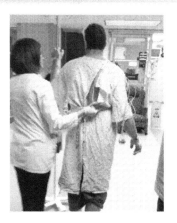

To: Adrienne Kallweit	CC: Christina
From: Kevin	
Subject: Re: Checking In	October 22, 2009 4:55 PM

Hi Adrienne,

Everything is going great. Christina and I have really banded together to make sure everything is running smoothly. I've honestly been operating as if you guys are still here. I've been talking with the franchisees as I usually do, calling sales leads and the big one, preparing for training next week.

I know it must be extremely difficult going through all of this, but please know everyone here as stepped it up to make sure SeekingSitters is still moving forward.

Tell David he looks great. If he's worried about work, tell him the word on the street is these SeekingSitters things can be run from home ☺

PS – newsletter will be out tomorrow.

It was motivating to hear from the office. A favorite saying throughout my life has been *Keep Moving Forward* and we have adopted this phrase as one of our company's mottos – so it was relieving to know that everything with SeekingSitters was *moving forward* as normal....it started to help me feel normal. It took me away from the noise of the monitors, the brain drain level checks, and constant worry.

Later that evening I posted an update on CaringBridge for the world to see. My posts on CaringBridge primarily gave an overview of the positive progress of the day as well as showed David's strength and humor – I didn't want to convey the stresses of the day for the world to see.

THURSDAY, OCTOBER 22, 2009 10:25 PM, CDT

David is still in ICU and will be for at least 6 more days. His fever has gone up some this evening, but they are monitoring it. They have to keep a cooling blanket on him and he HATES it! Keeps trying to escape from it. He asked to sit in a chair because he thought he could get away from it and then they laid it on top of him in the chair. The nurse said kidding, "you should be happy that we don't just put ice down your pants and under your arms." and he said "it feels like you did!"

He had great progress today because he was up and walking for a few steps.

139

Then immediately following that post I sent David a text message for only him to see:

> **DAVID**
> Oct 22, 2009 10:14 PM
>
> Today was up and down. You started strong, walking. Then tired and fever up at the end of day. I am just sitting by you.

I so much just wanted him to respond to me. The simple action of his response from a text message was gone.

Experiencing L O V E

CHAPTER THIRTEEN

LAPS AROUND
THE ICU

It is wonderful to have many friends, but you really only need one who can connect with you deeper than anyone else.

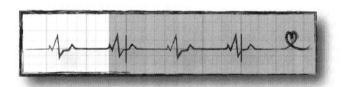

By that point I had checked out of the hotel and was living out of David's hospital room. It made no sense to have a hotel room that I wasn't spending any time in. I slept in a chair next to him and would doze on and off during the days and nights. David didn't sleep through the night anyway as the nurses were checking his vitals every hour and we were monitoring his brain drain levels as well as temperatures and other vitals. Plus I wanted to be there; he had asked me not to leave. The nurses thoughtfully didn't ask me directly as

143

you weren't allowed to *live* in the ICU.

In the mornings during non-visiting hours, I would walk to the gym a half a mile away, through the maze of hospital buildings. I knew my way around the hospital floors and the connecting corridors as if I had worked there for years. I would spend an hour working out at the gym and even though I wanted so much to disappear into my Lily Allen music and forget everything going on around me, I could never get my mind off of David and the fight for his healing. I would then shower, don dirty clothes and no makeup and head back to David's room while grabbing a coffee and breakfast sandwich on the way.

During the morning I would help him through physical therapy, bathing and meals and in between I would tend to some office work on my computer from my now "remote office." With 50 franchise locations depending on our support, our responses and presence were important. I tried to keep David updated on what was going on back at the office. He wanted so much to feel useful and be part of the day to day operations of the business. He would listen and at times drift off while I was talking to him about the latest news at the office.

During lunch, I would head down to the hospital cafeteria and grab a lunch, even pick up a few special requests for David and bring the treats back to his room for an afternoon snack. Whether he was craving ice cream or bananas I would help him. I wanted nothing but for him to get well. For our family to be back together.

His temperature was way down and he was tolerating the pain more and more and demanding less pain medicine. He would ask every nurse and doctor, "Can I leave yet?" and loved when he would get a rise out of the nurses.

That evening, he had a long walk throughout the ICU. As we made the rounds he said, "There are a lot of brain patients around here." The nurse and I laughed as we continued our walk around the hall. He even read a clock and held his balance pretty well. Even though he was improving, he continued to express his frustration about being in the hospital and strapped to the tubes and monitors. He wanted more than anything to push through and get better so he could get out of there. His determination to heal was unbelievable and all the family, the nurses and doctors, recognized his astounding improvements.

From the research I had been doing on his condition throughout the week I knew we weren't out of the clear on the mild to severe disabilities that could affect the body from any brain damage including paralysis, problems with thinking, problems with speaking and emotional problems. He struggled with walking, but he was unsteady mainly due to atrophy from lying in bed for so many days. But overall there appeared to be no paralysis. It was too early to start testing his cognition and his speech was still slightly impaired in part by the medications he was taking throughout the week. Regarding emotional problems – I wouldn't necessarily attribute his frustration of being in the hospital to emotional problems, as I wanted him to get out of there too.

But even with the unbelievable improvement, we understood he could experience these problems if he suffered a vasospasm. The vasospasm window was about to begin.

All of David's family had left by Friday evening and it was peaceful to be alone, just the two of us. Well, the two of us and a constant stream of nurses, doctors, beeping machines and tubes coming out of every end of his body.

That evening he wanted to write the CaringBridge message himself and I told him that I would have to type for him.

145

FRIDAY, OCTOBER 23, 2009 5:25PM, CDT

David just wanted me to send you all a message:

Been in here 3 days and I am going stir crazy and Adrienne won't let me get on my phone. The food is wonderful. (He said that sarcastically) Not to mention the staff here is...extraordinary, like a 5 star hotel. (sarcasm) I wish all of you could take such a fun two week self-induced vacation in the middle of your busy life someday. Nothing like waking up brushing your teeth and heading to the hospital. Thank you Megan and David for sending the chocolate strawberries - I didn't get any but they were handing them out to the waiting room and they looked really good. Hope to see you all soon.

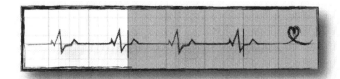

Saturday, October 24th was a great day of rest but it was also the first day of the vasospasm risk period. David's temperature was down to a normal level; he didn't have much pain medicine and was sleeping well. They started talking about possibly moving him out of the ICU Monday morning if they were able to remove the brain drain.

Around 6:00 p.m. David took the remote for the TV in his room and started flipping channels. The simple task of flipping stations on the TV was a monumental leap. He hadn't been able to hold the remote just 24 hours earlier. He stopped on a college football game, watched a few plays and then turned to me with a puzzled expression, "Why are there football games on a Wednesday?" I paused with concern, "David, it's Saturday." Even though he remembered details of family visits over the past three days and some events that took place, that TV football game was his first real memory of his space in time following surgery. He said he felt like he lost four days of his life.

During the evening non-visiting hours I went to eat dinner away from the hospital campus. The hospital is located adjacent to the Central West End of St. Louis with wonderful restaurants and walking paths. That particular evening I was in serious need of an adult beverage and was looking forward to some time to be alone and gather my thoughts after a very long week. I found the best little Mexican restaurant that I have visited every trip back to St. Louis, Tortillaria. They have the best tamales and salsa.

147

While alone at Tortillaria many thoughts raced through my head. David was improving but I continued to hold onto the fear of the "what-if" because there were still so many uncertainties. Just that day a patient across the hall from David, who came in the same day David did, died. I thought about how quickly things could turn.

While I was sitting there drinking my margarita and wrestling with these thoughts, I received a text on my phone. Message announcement popped up:

David is saved on my phone as "Love." As soon as I saw **Love** pop up it felt as if he had risen from the dead – like the person that I had been sitting bedside throughout the week was not even David, simply a hospital patient. Before I even read his message, tears began to well up in my eyes. It was an immediate feeling of relief to get a text message from him. Modern technology brought the greatest celebration of the week. I quickly opened the message he sent me:

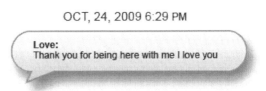

With a smile on my face and tears running down my cheeks, I wrote him back immediately:

LOVE
Oct 24, 2009 6:29 PM

Adrienne:
I love you so much. I am bawling in this restaurant. I love getting your text. Thank you. Thank you.

Love:
Don't cry. Get cards let's play gin. Since I cannot drink gin.

Adrienne:
If you can, call your mom.

Love:
Will call now

Adrienne:
I will get some cards and be back soon.

Through the phone there were no brain drains, tubes, needles, monitors – it was just David, my husband and best friend.

I helped the nurses in any way I could and was building a great relationship with many of them. Our favorite nurse by far was Mike, and David made an immediate connection with him. Mike would tell jokes to David and David would try to talk Mike into letting him sneak out of the hospital. A Chris Rock look alike as well as the quick-witted humor. Mike didn't take attitude from any of his patients.

149

While Mike first was assigned to David's room, David was having a very serious issue. He hadn't, well...hadn't had a poop all week and it was becoming a very serious situation. Mike was determined to make "it" happen for David. There were suppositories, liquids and more and more fluids to help him GO. Every time I would see Mike throughout the day I would ask, has it happened? And the answer was always NO. They had to set up a portable toilet in David's ICU room that did not offer any sort of privacy. You can just imagine "going" in a Johnny-on-the-spot that's made of glass set in the middle of the mall.

I headed out for my typical evening no-visiting hours. When I came back to the 11th floor and the double doors opened I gasped, "Oh good Lord!" I knew that Mike had made it happen.

At the room, Mike had two bottles of air freshener, one in each hand like loaded guns spraying all over every square inch of the room and David was already back in bed. Mike was proud of himself that he helped David get things moving and he was even more hilarious about his non-subtle way of letting everyone know that David had just stunk up the entire 11th floor.

It was only six days since the aneurysm and David was beginning to heal more rapidly than anyone's wildest imaginings. And for me, since receiving his text message the day before, I finally began to *see* his healing.

We went on a walk that day and all the nurses were staring at David. He asked the nurse who was walking with us, "Why is everyone looking at me like this?" and she replied, "We don't get many patients around here that talk back to us, let alone make laps around the neo-ICU."

David continued to push himself by walking further each day. During our walks, he would stop to look out the windows and ask questions about where the hospital was located and what direction we were facing. We knew the St. Louis area well from past family trips as well as territory map planning for the St. Louis franchisee. I knew he was longing to go outside and imagined how hard it was for him to be trapped inside the hospital walls.

David was in no condition to take a stroll through the park, but because of his improving condition Mike helped get clearance from his doctor to extend his excursions and we were allowed a little escape from the 11th floor that evening.

We went down the elevator with Mike to the first floor. David in his gown with IV pole pulling along next to him, a drain coming out of his head and bandages holding all the tubes in place. It wasn't a pretty sight, but hey, it was the hospital. We weren't going on a date night. As we got downstairs David walked around the atrium and looked at the fountain. Beside it was a little girl, about the same age as our youngest daughter, throwing pennies into the fountain. David – a big kid at heart himself – has always loved interacting with children and loves to hear them laugh and tell silly jokes. Since he was missing our children I could tell he wanted to say "hi" to her. He went up to the little girl and said, "Hi 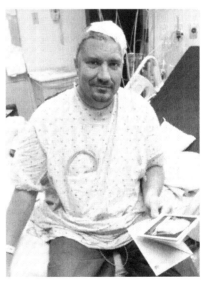 there." A completely sincere impulse, but not realizing that at the moment he didn't look like a friendly dad but rather a

scary Frankenstein. The little girl looked up at David, gasped and ran to her mommy, grabbing her leg and hiding behind her. The mom gave us a polite "I'm sorry" smile and David and I looked at each other, burst into laughter and immediately walked away. David said to me, "That was not a good idea." We continued to laugh and decided it would be best to head back upstairs where he fit in better – with the other bandaged patients.

As I sat there next to him that evening, grateful he was improving so rapidly, I had a strange thought. I began to wonder about our first post-brain surgery fight. I had been spending all my days praying for him to get well, wanting him to recover and being there to love him. But I also feared that we eventually would get back to life: Life with love, laughter and even dissention. As he was getting better and better I started thinking ahead, to the reality of life as it is – the human condition – and in a way started dreading it.

I shifted my thoughts to *the now* and posted information online about his great progress that day.

SUNDAY, OCTOBER 25, 2009 11:46PM, CDT

CARINGBRIDGE.ORG

David is doing great today. So much that he actually talked me into using his phone :) and is actually working right now. He is starting to understand the full scope of all of this and that patience is important in the healing process. He told me last night it just has been hard to understand why he has to stay in the hospital when he didn't choose to check in. Was hard for him to comprehend at first. His strength is amazing.

Thank you everyone for reaching out to us during this time. It has definitely been a hard strain on the family and please send many prayers as we move through this. Everyone is asking how I am making it - and the only way I can describe how I have made it though is that God has been carrying me.

I have faith that David will make a full recovery and hopefully David can give you an update himself tomorrow.

CHAPTER FOURTEEN

HALLOWEEN FIVE DAYS EARLY

Sometimes you have to throw traditional rules out the window and think outside the box. Create your own happiness.

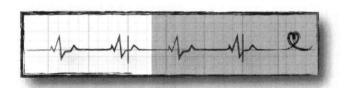

Because David was stable and improving, I decided it was safe to take a trip home to see the kids and take care of some work. It was the last week in October and I planned on taking the kids trick-or-treating for an early Halloween as the actual holiday was five days later. We arranged for David's sister Carol to come to the hospital and spend the week with him while I was home. He was fine with the arrangements and by that point was just determined to get

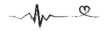

better and released from the hospital. I booked a flight to Tulsa.

At the airport it was very crowded and I had the unfortunate luck to be chosen as the randomly selected strip search candidate. I wouldn't be surprised if my disposition seemed a bit suspicious – anxious (to fly), nervous (for David) and traveling with no bags. The burly female TSA agent pulled me aside and asked me to unbutton my pants so they could feel behind the top of my jeans. I refused and stated that the intrusion was a violation of my personal space. They argued with me and said if I didn't unbutton my pants I would not be able to go through security or get on the plane. I asked for a supervisor. A man slightly resembling Ted Kaczynski came around the corner and said, "Ma'am, you are going to have to obey their orders or we will not allow you through. Or we can take you in a back room so we can do it there in private." I thought, *How did these people have any qualifications to force me to unbutton my pants and feel through my clothes?* I wanted to see some credentials. By then there were five TSA agents surrounding me and it felt like the zombie scene in the Michael Jackson "Thriller" video. I began losing my cool with the increased security moving in to violate me but I reluctantly unbuttoned my jeans.

The woman started feeling under the top band of my jeans, for where, I could only guess, they thought I would be hiding a bomb. That act triggered something in the deep recesses of my animal self because at that moment I started ranting (half hysterics, half crying) and said, "I can't believe you are doing this. My husband is dying in the Barnes Jewish Hospital and this <sniff..sniff> is a violation. What gives you the right? I don't have anything on me and I have been through so much this week." (Nothing I was saying made sense and, even more importantly, these idiotic strangers had no need to know about David's condition.) Ted interrupted my hysterics, "Ma'am, you are going to have to calm down." From the tone of his voice I could tell he was one finger push away from the irate passenger alarm button that would bring about my apprehension in the Lambert St. Louis International Airport. Still shaking with anger, I closed my mouth while they proceeded to dig through every inch of my purse, another violation, an area of someone's life that no stranger should be allowed free access into. What if they swiped something out of my purse during all the confusion? What a great scam those TSA agents have going! I was so angry, confused and feeling violated, and buttoned back up my pants, walked off sniffling and attempted to pull myself together before boarding the plane to Tulsa. I sat in a quiet spot to pray, think and chill out! The last thing I wanted was a dispute on the plane with the flight attendants.

I was thrilled to see our children. The school's teachers had been informed about David and allowed me to go directly to their classrooms to get all three kiddos. I gave each of them with a *longer than they wanted* hug in front of their entire classrooms – no one cared as we were relieved and excited to be together again. On the way home from school I told them we were going trick-or-treating that evening. They were at first confused and said, "But it's not Halloween." I explained to them that I wouldn't be home on Halloween so we could go early! They loved the idea of two Halloweens and were thrilled to dress up four days before the official Trick-o-Treat day.

As soon as we got home they raced to the costume box and picked out their favorite characters from the boxes of old Halloween costumes in the storage room. Bella pieced together three different princess costumes. Canaan put on the scariest costume he could find (even talking me into letting him use some fake blood we had in the box) and Ethan used his Flash Superhero costume from the Halloween prior.

All dressed up, we walked the neighborhood where the neighbors were confused and most of them didn't even have candy. I explained at every house why we were trick-or-treating early and once they heard the story they scurried through cupboards and pantries and candy dishes to find something, anything for the kids. A woman from one house gave them breath mints from out of her purse.

To make the time together happy and uplifting was my goal, as the kids had all been sad and stressed. Bella kept asking, "Is Daddy coming home this afternoon?" Canaan wanted to call Daddy every minute and Ethan had been overly sensitive, crying a lot. It was challenging to get all the hugs and conversations accomplished in that short trip. I caught Ethan writing a note to David on our bathroom white board. I gave him a big hug and then spent the evening talking to all the kids about David. They were all scared and I told them that I was too.

It was then that I realized the last memory Canaan recalled most of his Daddy was that horrible sight of David lying on the floor of our bathroom. And then his Daddy was gone. *How hard that would have been for him*, I worried. I talked with the kids every day that I was in St. Louis but seeing them and being with them showed me how hard it all was on our family.

I could only give them as many hugs and assurances that would fit into the few hours I was home, and promise them that Daddy would be coming home and that he was doing well. I then talked to them how important it was for them to pray for Daddy to get well.

They each said their prayers for Daddy. Canaan, who is our little preacher, "God, Please help Daddy in the hospital and get him well and thank you for the doctors and thank you for Mommy coming home." Ethan's turn was next and in his soft almost mumbling way of talking, "God, Help Daddy get well so we can play Legos." Bella was too nervous to pray and I told her that was OK and that she could pray in her heart. Then we all slept together in my bed that evening as no one wanted to be apart from one another.

The rest of my trip was spent taking care of business at the office. Before I went into the building I sat in my car and put my head on the steering wheel and prayed. I needed to be there 100% for our office team and for the

159

work that needed to be done over the next 24 hours. Again, I asked God for strength and to help me perform all the tasks that needed to be accomplished throughout the day.

It was refreshing to be around my work family. As employees have come and gone throughout the time of our business, in the natural evolution of a company, David and I have always felt blessed for people who have given of themselves to our company. We take value in their dedication and feel each person has a special part in our lives. We don't ask personal faith questions of our employees but through our day to day conversations I know our office team has a strong faith. It was likely they prayed for their own personal strength during David's absence.

When I was home we didn't waste time becoming confused or feeling lost without David. Rather, we conquered tasks with success. We hosted a company dinner, facilitated a new franchise location training, and planned for the upcoming weeks' tasks. We utilized every minute of my visit with amazing productivity.

The kids and I talked on the phone with David that evening and then I talked with Carol who had an update from the doctors, explaining they had an angiogram performed to see the status of the aneurysm as well as evaluate his risk for vasospasm. Carol explained some of the test, "They did the angiogram to look at the arteries in his head." As the kids sat closely next to me they could hear Carol on the call. Canaan said, "What are arteries?" "Arteries are blood vessels that carry oxygen and nutrients to the body." They all looked at me with a dazed expression. "Well, they put a tube through his leg that shoots a special dye in his head so that they can see the vein that was broken to make sure it healed." Their confused expressions changed to amazement and all said in unison,

"Oooowwwweeee." Carol could hear the kids in the background and began to laugh at their response.

Carol said the angiogram revealed good news about his healing so after I tucked the kids in their beds I updated every one on David's progress through the CaringBridge website and then packed my bags for my early morning flight back to St. Louis.

TUESDAY, OCTOBER 27, 2009 4:52PM, CDT

CARINGBRIDGE.ORG

David has had a hard Monday/Tuesday – many tests & the angiogram revealed that he is at a low chance of spasm (good news!); however, they identified a blood clot in his leg. This is not super serious and they are treating it with a filter that will help stop any blood clots getting to his heart.

I heard from his doctor Monday night and the Dr. was extremely encouraging – which was great because his doctor does not sugar coat anything and this is really the first time he has been really encouraging about his progress. He said that David is doing extremely well with all he went through. It is just a miracle what the doctors can do and how strong the body is to heal from something like this.

David actually called home Monday night to check on us and was really verbal and sounded like himself. He also had a cat scan and it looked good. His sister is with him at the hospital and Carol said that the Dr. said that he will be in ICU through next Monday (November 2nd) and then we will see how long he will be in a normal room. They are doing lots of monitoring to keep him well for a long life ahead of him.

Experiencing LOVE

CHAPTER FIFTEEN

THE KIDS NEEDED ME

Always think before you speak. Never react when you are too glad, too mad or too sad.

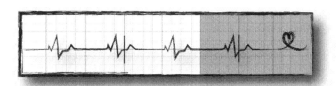

I had quickly resumed my hospital routine in St. Louis since getting back from Tulsa, helping David throughout the day. Morning workout, afternoon lunch, taking time to work on my computer, sitting by his bed and praying for healing. He was getting stronger, had his stitches in his head removed and was even walking around everywhere but his legs were very stiff and he still had the brain drain in his head. The doctors said that would be David's last week in the ICU but they couldn't let him leave without having the drain removed. In order to remove the brain drain they needed to start raising the level of the drain which meant his body had to work harder on its own to

163

drain the fluid, hopefully reabsorbing it on its own. If they were able to continue to raise the drain without much pain, they would try to clamp it for 24 hours the following day to see if he could tolerate it and start reabsorbing the fluids on his own.

It was an excruciating procedure – every time they raised the levels David would agonize with the pain. Determined to move forward in his healing, he tolerated the pain as best as he could. Reabsorbing the fluid on his own was of course the best route for him; however, if he couldn't tolerate it they would have to place a shunt in his brain to help drain the fluids. It is a common procedure for someone in his condition and it wouldn't compromise his quality of life, but I was concerned as it would require a lifetime of monitoring and maintenance.

Even though David was doing so well, talking to all the nurses and even doing some work throughout the day, they continued constantly to test his neurological state every few hours with the same questions. "WHERE ARE YOU?" and "WHAT IS YOUR NAME?" His favorite joke was to yell the answers as loud as the nurses would ask the questions, almost mocking the stupidity of the questions. He even asked, "Can you please ask me something else?" after getting frustrated at having to answer these same questions over and over so she asked him to recite the Greek alphabet and the pledge of allegiance – which of course he did, getting a laugh out of the nurse while doing so. The nurse then said, "We aren't used to our patients talking so much here in ICU!" David began having a much better attitude about being in the hospital, coming to terms with having patience with his healing process.

That evening while I was working and David was resting, Nurse Mike made an interesting comment. He had been observing David and me interact throughout the past several days and was curious about our relationship. "You guys get along real well." I looked up from my computer,

"Thanks, Mike." He opened up a little to us, "My wife and I aren't getting along well, and I have been amazed watching you both over the past couple weeks." David and I were surprised that he had been observing our relationship and completely humbled that he wanted to talk to us. Looking my way first, perhaps seeking my permission to reveal more about us, David said, "Well, we love each other and work hard to make sure our relationship stays strong." He emphasized, "Especially after we started a family. It was really hard on our marriage." As he walked around David's bed changing the fluid bags hanging above his head, Mike added, "Yeah, it has been hard since we have had our baby. She is now one." David continued, "Something we do is to have date night every week. It isn't always easy because we are so busy, but we work hard at trying to make that happen. Most of all, we are best friends." David glanced towards me and I gave him a warm smile.

I drew back from the conversation and listened to David talk with Mike. In that ironic moment of David helping Mike, the nurse who assisted in David's own life-saving journey, I began to see how God's plan is bigger than we can even comprehend.

Dr. Chicoine visited David's room that evening and spent quite a bit of time answering our questions and talking to us about David's condition. He reassured us that there aren't specific reasons why people have aneurysms and it's actually more common than you think for people to have an aneurysm, but not all aneurysms rupture. He said that David likely had the aneurysm for many years, but not taking his high blood pressure medication the weekend prior to the rupture could have triggered the episode. (During a conversation with one of his doctors a few days earlier, David revealed that he had forgotten to take his blood pressure medicine during the weekend at The Farm.) Dr.

Chicoine said due to the very deformed shape of the aneurysm he may have to have a subsequent surgery to put a path (like a crutch) through the vein to help the blood flow and prevent another rupture. He said they would not very likely have to do that but they would keep a close eye on the vein for months and years to come to make sure it is functioning properly. "Over time David will be able to lead a normal life, but he is not going to be able to play full contact football!" (A brain surgeon's way of lightening the mood.) He said it's likely David would have the shunt and surgery is already scheduled. "We'll continue to watch the drainage and there's a chance that surgery will be cancelled but we'll keep an eye on it." He directed his final comments to David, "Care of yourself following surgery, such as exercise and proper medication, will help your quality of life. We'll do another CT scan this weekend to see how your veins are doing."

Most of all, Dr. Chicoine was positive about David's progress, saying several times in the conversation that he could not have predicted how well David would have done with the kind of bleed he had, almost expressing surprise with David's miraculous recovery. Then I knew what they couldn't tell us in those first hours after we arrived at Barnes Jewish, how they didn't have optimistic expectations for David's outcome. But now their thoughts and predictions were proved wrong.

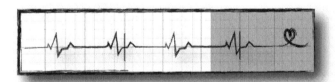

It was Halloween. A family holiday favorite, with hay rides and costume contests at home. I wanted to get our minds off of the vasospasm period count down and try to focus on some fun for the holiday. My cousin, Mary, who lived in St. Louis and was coincidentally a patient of Dr. Chicoine's several years earlier, came up to the hospital and brought some costumes for us — Elvira and Frankenstein — which the nurses loved. She also brought Halloween decorations for the room and we went trick or treating through the ICU walkways. It felt as if we were in a real-life haunted house! It was great to laugh together and have a little reminder of life outside the hospital.

SATURDAY, OCTOBER 31, 2009

CARINGBRIDGE.ORG

Happy Halloween!

We are still in ICU, just waiting and waiting. And the nurses are really getting sick of David - David keeps getting out of his bed on his own, unplugging the monitors etc. when he wants to do something. The nurse gave him a lecture about how she needs to do it and then said "don't upset the hand that feeds you!" Ha!

He has the brain drain clamped today (testing to see if it will work on its own) and he is doing OK. This is the test to see if he has to have the shunt implanted on Monday or if he can manage his own draining. We hope for draining on his own - but it is just a wait and see.

Kids are really missing daddy! They are coming up to St. Louis tomorrow to see him and David is anxious to see them too. David is working today and watching Nebraska football - baby steps of life getting back to normal.

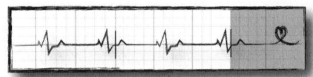

David and I were spending the morning of November 1st reading emails and he was even working some on his phone. Even though the office was handling all the operations, he wanted to feel productive and checked in to the Tulsa SeekingSitters' operations. I was sitting next to David and could tell he was getting frustrated, "What is wrong?" He explained that the office had assigned a sitter to a family that he thought they shouldn't have assigned. I told him that it is OK and I know they are handling things well and I am sure they verified the arrangements. He got more frustrated and mouthed off to me, "This is so frustrating being in here not able to do anything. You can't relate. It is not like you have had a hard past two weeks. I want to be out of here." My breath stopped as I thought to myself, *Did he really just say that? These past two weeks of stress and holding it all together. Thoughts of mentally planning my husband's funeral and being a widow and taking the burden of raising our three kids alone and operating the business alone...alone...alone – does he not understand what this has done to ME TOO!* I put my head down and prayed right then and there. *God, Please do not let me get angry at this comment, he knows not what he says, he knows not what he says.* I kept repeating that through my head.

As calmly as I could muster out, "David, do you know how serious all of this is?" He said, "Yeah, sure. I just want to get out of here." From his cynical and off-putting response I realized he had no idea how serious things had been, still were and how close he was even at that moment to dying. I knew it was time to tell him. Before then, we hadn't really let David in on the depth of his injury, how close he was to death and even the lingering vasospasm risk. As he said on his way into brain surgery, "Why the worry, it isn't like I'm having brain surgery." I knew all along he didn't know the depth of the injury and I knew it was time for him to understand.

I didn't say anything more. My silence worried him. I grabbed my computer and pulled up my previous search on "subarachnoid hemorrhage aneurysm." There they were again, those heart-stopping statistics the same as two weeks earlier when I had no clue what any of David's brain problem was all about.

I handed the computer to David and asked him to read the pages online and left the room. I was speechless from his earlier comment and I had to walk to blow off the steam. I went to the hospital bookstore. They brewed Starbucks there and although it wasn't staffed with Starbucks baristas and they couldn't make my double tall dry non-fat cappuccino, it was close enough to the real thing to get my daily fix.

I grabbed my coffee and a random book off the shelf and headed to the back of the bookstore. I took a seat and sat there in shock reflecting on his words. I thought to myself, *I have been sitting next to David for the past two weeks, fighting for him to survive and finding a way to survive myself. And he disparaged everything that I had experienced.*

I reached out to the friend that had been with me all week for help. *God, Help me through this moment. I am so upset and I don't want to be upset at David because he didn't mean to hurt me.*

In my heart I felt His message, just as I had heard it in David's stinky truck and in the emergency room in Tulsa. **Go home. David is healing and it is time for you to go home and be with your kids. They are the ones who need you now.**

The kids did need me. I felt what I needed to do and

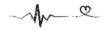

I had peace with the answer. I wasn't upset with David's comments at all. My mom was already scheduled to bring up the kids to visit Daddy at the hospital and with one quick call, the plans to go back home were arranged.

When I came back to David's room it had been about an hour since I left and during that time he had not only read the article that I handed him but he started asking nurses detailed questions about his condition and all that he had gone through. They explained how serious his situation was and still is. They also explained that many of the patients that check into the 11th floor never make it out or are transferred into assisted living communities and never get back to a normal way of life.

It was the stark truth about his close encounter with Death. He apologized to me for the comment he made but I told him he didn't need to apologize – that it made me see it was time for me to go home. He said he didn't want me to leave but understood that if I felt that was the best option, he would respect my decision. I went on to explain how well he is doing and that his sisters can come be with him as they have been offering their support. I explained that I needed to be with our children, they are aching and need to be with me and I explained that I didn't know how long I was going to be gone but I could be back immediately if he needed me.

We decided that when my mom arrived she would stay the night with the kids so they could see Daddy and then we would leave the next morning. We arranged for David's sisters to be with him throughout the duration of his hospital stay.

The kids' visit was scary and overwhelming for them. They didn't fear that Daddy was dying because he was alive and talking to them so that didn't enter their minds. Seeing, feeling, touching, and hugging Daddy helped resolve many of their fears about him dying. But it was scary for them to see all the tubes and monitors that were keeping

him alive hooked up to their Daddy. Ethan didn't want to hug Daddy and glanced from afar. (Later he told us that he thought Daddy looked like an alien and that is why he didn't want to be close to him.) Canaan, our oldest, had lots of questions about how each contraption worked and when he would be coming home. Bella, our youngest, simply hugged Daddy and told him she missed him.

It was a good visit because we knew he was coming home and we could assure each of them of that news when they said goodbye.

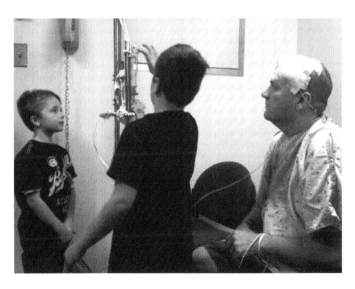

CHAPTER SIXTEEN

PREPARING FOR
DADDY'S RETURN

It has been told that in life you will create a "new normal" for yourself at least five times. Embrace every "new normal" and own it. Don't mourn for the "old normal" but rather let it remain as a sweet place in your memory.

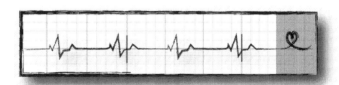

I left David at the hospital and returned to life back home. It was hard for me to be there without him and return to our day-to-day life with no husband, father or business partner.

I had to figure out how to handle many of the things that he typically took care of at home and with the business. Things that I just naturally leaned on him for support were now my responsibility. Only a few days had passed but already they were constant reminders of what it would have been like if David had not made it through the aneurysm. I had to stay focused on the fact that he did make it through, that he would be coming home and that we would find our new normal.

I continued with work, not taking any time off during that trip back home. Not knowing what to expect of my needed attention when he was finally released from the hospital, I needed to make sure everything was in order with the business. It was a surreal feeling to have just left the ICU, tending to lifesaving devices and shifting to the priorities of work and home life.

The time with me home was also hard on the kids. They didn't see Daddy healing and their last memory of him was Daddy (the alien) strapped to tubes and in a wheelchair. We would call him on his cell phone as often as we could. I tried to keep life normal for them, with school, football practice, and play dates with friends.

But it was especially hard on Ethan. He kept most of his fear and sadness inside and although I tried to talk to him often about what he was feeling he just wanted Daddy to come home. We all did.

Back in St. Louis, his sisters, who each spent two days at the hospital, were helping David on his path to getting stronger every day. As the baby of the family, his big sisters had always been very protective of David which made them wonderful caretakers in the healing time.

He made a few updates on the CaringBridge site on his own and to my surprise, while I was home David called a good friend of mine and asked her to come and take me to lunch. I was thankful for his strength and for his love for me and for those around him. I was thankful that the bitterness of being in the hospital, for his time lost, was quickly changing to appreciation for his life.

TUESDAY, NOVEMBER 3, 2009 7:38 PM, CST

CARINGBRIDGE.ORG

Hello all and thank you for all of your support and prayers. It is Tuesday lying in bed listening to fox news. The procedures have all gone well. I am praying to get out of ICU tomorrow and home by Sat. I am sure the Dr.'s will let me go when I am ready. I really am feeling better every day. Actually my back side feels worse than my head from just laying here and not being active. Missing the kids a lot. The nurses tell me it is nice to take care of someone that talks back to them in a coherent manner. They have all been truly wonderful. Reading through the messages has been great and has brought tears to my eyes many of you asked what can you do to help. Give Adrienne a call just to talk have coffee or a girls night yes Adrienne you deserve a kitchen pass I will be home soon and again thanks for all of your prayers.
Love you all.
David

We got news that David was scheduled to be transferred out of the ICU and into a regular patient room on November 5th. His body wasn't able to drain the fluids from his brain on its own so they scheduled surgery to install a shunt and would move him out following the surgery.

Surgery to install the shunt was successfully completed and they removed all drains and catheters, leaving a single IV in his arm, and moved him into a regular room.

David called me on Saturday to tell me that his sister was going to sneak him out of his room so they could walk to her hotel room and watch the Nebraska-OU football game. I offered him, "Good luck with that," as I imagined his naked butt walking through the halls of Barnes Jewish Hospital. I got a call the next day that the escape plan was successful and they watched the football game from her hotel room and she even got him some O'Doul's to drink during the game. As much as it saddens me to say, I was glad that his alma mater, Nebraska, beat my alma mater, Oklahoma, in that monumental football game. David deserved that victory celebration!

Our last final hurdle, the vasospasm risk, was scheduled to end on Monday. Clearing that window with positive vitals meant being released. The waiting period was stressful as he had improved so vastly but we knew he could potentially face a major setback.

David heard a rumor from one of his nurses that he wasn't going to come home to a rehabilitation facility but rather straight to our house. Throughout the hospital stay, we heard over and over that David would need rehabilitation, possibly a extended care facility or out-patient care when returning to Oklahoma, so I wanted to hear the doctor's orders directly. Even if that was the case, we still weren't sure of his at-home needs or if he would have daily physical therapy appointments. I could tell he was improving and his pain medications were being reduced daily, so he was more alert every time we spoke. He said his head felt great and that he had been walking a lot, even going outdoors on Sunday with his sister.

It had been sixteen days since the aneurysm and four days into his stay in the regular hospital room when I got the victorious news that he cleared the vasospasm risk! He was going to be released! The kids and I celebrated and I made plans to head to St. Louis and bring him home.

It was a drab and dreary drive to St. Louis. It rained the entire trip but as soon as I neared Barnes Jewish Hospital the sight of the building glistening in the rain lifted my heart; the place where my husband's life was saved.

I arrived at his room at about 5:00 p.m. and when I saw him I could hardly believe my eyes. He was next to his bed waiting for me, standing unassisted, without the brain drain or IVs protruding from his body. He looked very healthy, having lost nearly fifteen pounds. His stitches were removed and his hair had slightly grown back. The scar that went across half of his head wasn't as noticeable as when I left just five days earlier. His eyes lit up at the sight of me, as they always have done, and I stood before him taking in the miracle for a moment. *I had my David back!* I threw my arms around him and hugged and kissed him as if we had been apart for years. I stepped back and looked at him again. The time away allowed me to see his amazing progress. "David, it is all just a miracle."

As he got back in his hospital bed, I asked if he wanted me to climb in next to him. An affirmative "Yes!" and I nestled close by his side. We hadn't been able to get this close to one another for three weeks and we were enjoying the moment talking, playing cards and scrolling through TV channels...that is until a nurse kicked me out of

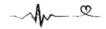
the bed! We laughed for getting in trouble in this unusual predicament.

The next morning while we waited for the discharge papers I posted on CaringBridge.

David Comes Home Today!!!!!!!! We will be driving back home around noon. David is doing GREAT - he is off his IV, not in a lot of pain and even showering on his own. He walked down 3 flights of stairs with me yesterday and has been walking all over the hospital this week with his sisters while I was gone.

He is so positive and ready to get back to life! He misses the kids so much and they are ready to have their daddy back too! (They are at home making him a welcome home banner & making up a welcome home song for him.)

He had the shunt put in last week so they will continue to monitor this and do regular checkups to make sure he is Healing OK. The doctors have said he falls in the 15% of people that have had a cranial aneurysm with a Subarachnoid and survive with all cognition, motor skills and headed for 100% recovery.

This journey has been unbelievable. I have heard people say before that "life is so fragile" but I think anything but that now after watching David's strength through this I have learned that although life can change or be gone in an instant, a life is anything but fragile. We fight to live and I have watched David's strength through this, he even gives me strength as I have needed it, and I am so amazed at him, as we all are. I count my blessings every minute of every day...

David had been incessantly asking the nurses, "Can I leave yet?" and around 10:00 a.m. they finally gave us discharge papers and signed David out of the hospital. There was one sheet of paper, resembling the office visit slip you receive from your primary care physician. "Please sign here. The pink copy is yours." And that was it.

David and I looked at each other in confusion. There were no instructions, bottles of post-aneurysm pills to swallow, precautions to take with the new shunt, or dire warnings about the metal clips in his brain setting off the metal detector at the airport. No physical therapy schedule. No orders for extended care. *That was it?* All the time he was in the hospital various doctors and nurses told us over and over he would likely receive physical therapy at a local hospital or treatment at an out-patient care center. Then we were just told, "Go home. Bye." It was surreal.

We asked if we could talk to Dr. Chicoine. I had thought of a list of questions during my drive to St. Louis and jotted them down when I arrived at the hospital:

> *Will he have another aneurysm if he coughs?*
> *How much can he lift?*
> *Can the kids get rowdy around him?*
> *What about exercise?*
> *What about his high blood pressure?*
> *What medicine should he take?*

David's list consisted of one important question:

Is it OK for me to ever drink beer again?

We were advised to call Dr. Chicoine's office with any questions as he would not be coming by David's room before we checked out. We tried to call his office from the hospital but were unable to reach him as he was in surgery...working on another brain patient. We looked at

179

each other and shrugged, "I guess we just go."

That really was it. Three weeks after it all had begun, we walked out of the hospital with our check-out slip that said David was healed.

On the seven-hour drive home we had a lot of time to talk about life and what we'd experienced over the past three weeks. I told him detailed accounts of what happened while he was in the hospital. He had forgotten some events due to the massive amounts of pain medicine. He loved hearing about his funny encounters with nurses, especially the hour following surgery when he did the countdown and ordered me to get his socks and shoes.

He and I had such a different journey over the preceding three weeks. I asked him how he stayed so strong through it all and he told me, "I just knew all along it wasn't my time."

I had so many hours to think about life and what it would be like after he came home during my weeks in the hospital, on plane trips between St. Louis and Tulsa, and over the course of three seven hour drives. During those moments I spent most of my time praying, reflecting on how thankful I was but I would also think about what we should do after we returned from the experience. *Should we shift our life direction? Should we change our entrepreneurial path to lessen the stress in our life?* I really didn't feel compelled to do these things but thought, *Maybe this experience is a sign to make a change in our life. Does David feel this way?*

Driving home we played a game I bought to play at the hospital that we had never opened. It was a thought-provoking game that asked questions like, "Would you rather live in a boat or a travel trailer?" or "If you were given a million dollars what would you do with it?" I thought it would be a good game to bring out David's cognitive skills and get his brain working again. (Little did I know his brain never stopped working!)

We played a few rounds and had some good laughs with the silly questions. Then David drew a question for himself, "If you could change what you are doing and pick any occupation or career or talent and immediately receive success, what would it be?"

I instantly got chills because I had wanted to ask him that question, but not that soon – the day he was leaving the hospital. I perked up to hear his answer.

Without hesitation and with a slight shake of his head, as if it was a silly question, he answered, "I would be doing exactly what I am doing now." Immediately I chimed in, "You mean even if you could do anything else in the world, you would be doing exactly what we are doing right now?" He answered unequivocally, "Yes." Of course in my *Let's talk about this for an hour even though it is absolutely unnecessary because the decision has already been made* sort of way that I like to handle topics, I pursued, "You mean even with all that we have just experienced, you don't think we should be driven to do something different in our careers, or make a drastic life change?"

He answered simply and softly, "Adrienne, I love what I do. I love my life with you. I love our kids. I love our home. I love our business. Every day in the hospital, I thought about the life we have and it made me want to fight harder and harder so that I could just return to it. I thank God I am able to do that."

He was right. We simply needed to focus on *moving forward*.

CHAPTER SEVENTEEN

OUR FIRST
FIGHT

Life is a long strand of events in which each event leads us to the next destination or a final destination. Every event is important. Don't take any moment for granted.

Depending on the research, David falls into either the 3% or 15% of all subarachnoid hemorrhage cranial aneurysm patients who have survived the injury and had full recovery – with either statistic, it is miraculous. He has no post-aneurysm side effects, either motor or cognitive, and he was even able to resume work about two weeks following the release from the hospital in St. Louis. We do not take

the incredible recovery for granted and pray with and for those who have a lost a loved one or have lifelong complications due to this same injury.

I kept a close eye on his cognitive skills at first and would perk up if he said something not quite right or remembered an event from our past a bit differently than my recollection. It was a Spanish Inquisition if he got something wrong. The ironic thing is that his memory for specific event details was better than mine before the aneurysm and is still today. It is unbelievable that David recalls much of his experience, with only bits and pieces missing.

After David's return from St. Louis, we celebrated his 41st birthday with a family party at our home and a few days later he returned to his normal workload of Monday billing for the local SeekingSitters' office, territory development for the franchise system, and office trainings. Even though we all loved to hear his laughter and feel his positive spirit in the office, we had to often force him to go home and rest like the doctor ordered. He was also instructed that he wasn't supposed to drive but started driving about two weeks after his discharge. The progress was primarily because he couldn't stand me driving him around one more day!

People around us couldn't believe his recovery. A church friend was shocked to see David at his desk working away when she dropped food for our family at the office! We had to contact the church to remove his name from the church bulletin prayer list, as he was sitting there every Sunday, healthy and attentive in the balcony pew.

The only thing he struggled with was his physical strength. He wanted to push himself to get stronger but his doctor advised him that he should lift no more than two pounds until the four week follow-up angiogram confirms successful healing. That was crazy because within days home he had carried much more. How could he not carry his thirty pound baby girl to bed!? Before the surgery, David could qualify for one of those Strong Men competitions. (I'd like to think.) He built a block wall in front of our house with his bare hands. But doc was right – his strength was definitely compromised by the aneurysm and he would get fatigued much easier than before. It would frustrate him and he eagerly awaited the four week follow-up in St. Louis. He wanted a peek inside to identify if it was safe to push himself and regain his strength.

The angiogram was at 8:00 a.m. on December 7th and his excitement to see the results prompted us to show up at 6:40 a.m. We had Bella with us for the trip and she was a trooper, getting up with us and walking to the hospital in the dark! When we got to the waiting area, the lights weren't even turned on and we laughed about our predicament. They took him in for the test on time and within an hour the doctor was visiting his room to give us the results.

Dr. Chicoine personally came to see us and give us the update. As we knew about Dr. Chicoine, he definitely doesn't sugarcoat anything and is a serious man, definitely good characteristics for a brain surgeon! He said to David, "Everything looks great and it is very *very* unlikely this will reoccur." We couldn't believe our ears. We were ecstatic! I will never forget him saying **very** twice. He continued, "We want to see you back in a year to do another angiogram to make sure all looks good." (A year later we returned for the second follow-up angiogram. The results were even more impressive. A complete medical release and a third follow-up scheduled in five years.)

David said in the months following the first angiogram, that he felt somewhat like Superman – invincible from a life-threatening injury and therefore able to tackle anything. But as time passed and having spoken to many who have lost loved ones or have personally been affected by this same injury, he wonders why his life was saved and

185

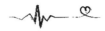

why he achieved full recovery. He believes that the answer will reveal in time and for now he accepts that he was given a blessing beyond his understanding.

Our personal life picked back up where we left off. Actually, when I think about it, I don't think our life really ever stopped. But following our return home, not a day went by that I didn't reflect on what could have been. If he had died, or returned home unable to walk or speak, or worse to me – lost his sense of humor or all cognitive ability. I went back to those moments in that special procedures waiting room in Tulsa and my depressed thoughts planning David's funeral. I almost lost him and I couldn't get that off of my mind.

It's not at all that I dwelt on the fear, nor was I depressed about the "what-if," but the little things made me pause. Like decorating for Christmas time that year. David always decorates the tree with the kids. He has done it every year and it is an activity that I do not have the patience to deal with – three kids buzzing around attempting to help assemble a prickly plastic tree and hang precious glass keepsakes that will shatter the instant their little impatient hands drop them. We agreed many Christmases earlier that he decorates the tree and I do the rest of the house. It has become a special time together. They erect our plastic beauty and then line the tree with mismatched ornaments from family and the kids are class treasures.

Just days after the first angiogram follow-up, the children and their Daddy were decorating the tree, *moving forward* as if nothing had happened over the past month. I thought to myself, *I wonder if that tree would have even gone up this year had David not survived* – and immediately offered my *Thank You* to God.

Our first date night out was on New Year's Eve. We celebrated with friends and danced the night away, *moving forward* with plans made many months before the aneurysm. At midnight we toasted our glasses to the year ahead. I looked up to him for our midnight kiss and thought how differently that evening could have been. With watery eyes, whispered in his ear, "I am so thankful you are here."

As life was *moving forward*, we were also reminded that the old stresses surrounding our life were right where we left them. While sitting by David in the hospital during the second week of our ordeal, I feared our first fight. I now think it stemmed more from fear of life resuming to normal and us forgetting the miracles we witnessed. David and I have had very few intense fights for a couple that spends nearly 24-7 together. With both of us being pretty strong minded, we are bound to get into a few squabbles. So by a "fight" I mean more of a conversation in which we are passionately discussing our own positions in a slightly louder tone than we would normally use with to each other. Let's just call it an argument for argument's sake.

It was unavoidable. We did have that first argument following the aneurysm. It happened on an ordinary stress-filled day and without even remembering how apprehensive I was about that inevitable marital tiff, there we were, all blown up like a festering boil. But within minutes I remembered - *this is DAVID, I almost lost him and he is here*

187

with me! What is more important than that?! I ignored the chance to get in the last word, and yielded to him.

A few months later there came the second verbal clash, and I was a little less inclined to drop the argument with the miracle of recovery not so fresh on my mind. Even though I didn't totally abandon the disagreement, I noticed as we began to state our respective cases that I wasn't inclined to continue the argument and was much more respectful and compassionate in our discussions. It just didn't seem 'worth it' to draw out an argument and miss precious time together that we could spend getting along. Even though we still have disagreements, this same subdued, low-intensity feeling has continued ever since.

One Sunday, nearly a year after David's aneurysm, David and I attended our Sunday school class after having a squabble when leaving the house. (Of course, the subject is now forgotten and was inconsequential, or I would have remembered it!)

One of our church's associate pastors, Reverend Ryan Moore, was a guest speaker. Ryan takes a pragmatic approach to scripture so that what he offers up in his presentation is realistic and relatable to our lives. I was enthusiastic to see his 6'6" stature commanding the Sunday school class's attention. David and I walked in a few minutes late due to the morning chaos; I hoped our body language didn't reveal the frustrations towards one another. We took a seat across from Henry (whom you met earlier in the book) and his wife Katherine.

I then grew even more excited when I realized the discussion topic of the day: Marriage Relationships. As we walked in, Ryan was candidly speaking about how he saw, "the downfall of marriages in our country was the failure of the husband to assume the leadership role model in the family, as the Holy Bible clearly enforces." I perked up to hear that we had arrived at the perfect moment in the lesson, discussing the husband's faults. *Maybe his lesson will support my argument and David will see that I am right.* (Whatever it was we were squabbling about.) But to my surprise, the lesson did the opposite. It diffused our argument and gave us a deeper understanding why we are able to make it through ***obstacles*** in our marriage.

Ryan went on to discuss the importance of the husband's role in the marriage in contrast to the wife's role. "The husband should show love and the wife should offer respect, as stated in Ephesians 5."

Ryan explained that he felt when the husband is strong in his faith it is more likely that there is strength in the marriage. The family, and the family's house, is like the church: Christ is the head of the church, and likewise, in Christ's name, the husband is the head of the family, the head of his house. Both the husband and wife have very important responsibilities for a successful marriage.

As Ryan spoke I realized how ridiculous I had acted towards David that morning. I then became grateful to God for the husband that I am blessed to have. I felt compelled to compliment David before the class following my not so kind words during our early morning argument, "I do believe this, as David has a deep faith that always gets us through any obstacle we are up against."

We smiled at each other and the argument (whatever it may have been) melted away and under the table, covertly, we clasped each other's hand.

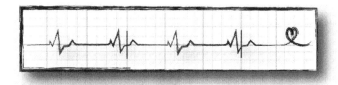

David's life-threatening experience, miraculous healing and second chances he received, didn't necessarily cause us to drastically change the course of our lives nor did it automatically erase every normal-life feeling. What it did absolutely do is provide us both a bigger perspective on how to approach issues in all aspects of our life and how to focus on what really matters in life, during this short time we are here on Earth.

Your time is precious; spend more of it with the people you love. We have an understanding that the time we have on Earth is definitely precious and to guard that time carefully. The block of time I have for my family, which includes church and prayer, and the block of time I have for work, leaves me a limited yet important time for friends and personal needs. I make sure that I spend this select time wisely with people who are special in my life.

As David reminded me on our drive home from St. Louis, spend your time doing what you love and do it with passion. We have a new perspective on life and how we handle our work and life balance. We still give everything we can to our careers but family always does come first and we make sure to keep this focus.

When in strife or in desperation, always remember to pray, every day. Since the aneurysm, I pray every day – whether it is for support, thanks, or for mere communication – I reach out to God through prayer. Just as Joli encouraged the Moms in the Monday Bible study – I now consider God as my best friend.

Experiencing L O V E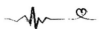

My son Canaan, now ten years old, has been asking a lot of questions about faith, about what is going to happen to him after he dies, and expressing worries about dying. I try as best as I can to answer him honestly and openly. But sometimes I explain, "You just have to have faith." I can tell him with honesty, "I believe in God and know that when we pray, God listens."

Before the events that occurred with David in the fall of 2009, I too struggled with the same questions Canaan was asking me, about knowing God is *for real* and having blind faith in Him. Even though I recognized God, believed I was going to heaven after I died, even though my faith had grown deeper throughout the years, I many times questioned God's validity and our Earthly purpose.

When I was five months pregnant with our first child, David and I had only been married for fifteen months. My very hormonal pregnancy caused me to start questioning life and what the heck we are all doing in this world. I basically flat out freaked out! I spent many days in anxiousness and doubt and my fear of death was intense. David would comfort me as I cried and say, "Adrienne, everything will be fine." He really didn't know exactly what to say at that point to his overly emotional pregnant bride, mainly because he essentially didn't get it! His outlook was and is, "We live, we die and we go to Heaven. What is the big deal?"

David's faith is solid and true and always has been. His faith is unlike my full range journey of asking questions: *What is the meaning of life? What really happens when I die?* or struggling with the question of *"Why Believe?"* To

193

him it is just a given, not a question. With that solid foundation, his outlook on life brings contentment and he is a contented man. He has worldly fears, a terrible fear of heights, and he struggles with the stresses of a growing family and growing business, but his faith in God is and always has been solid.

I had wanted more, however, and used to pray to God that he would **show** me a sign or reveal Himself to me so that I would know that he was *really there* and that my prayers were purposeful and that I should continue my faith. I know this was quite a large order to ask, but I recalled a story my mom told me many times growing up. She felt God revealed Himself to her during a time in her life when she was also struggling with the concept of faith as a young mother and wife and she was feeling alone and abandoned. She at first tried to find answers through worldly solutions, but when that failed, turned purposefully toward religion. She found all of the definitions she could find of the word faith and wrote them out on paper and posted them throughout the house, in attempts to absorb the literal definition of faith into her being. She kept these pages posted for six months until every single synonym and definition was memorized – but she said it didn't do any good, that "Faith is believing in things unseen," still didn't make sense to her. Then one dark early morning she was seated at her vanity with just a dim child's night-light emitting a faint glow. As she hid her face in her hands in complete angst, she felt a pressure on her left shoulder, like someone's hand pressing firmly. She uncovered her face to see who it was, and there was no one, nothing there except for a brilliant, pure white illumination that had no source except for its aura and it surrounded her, not like any physical thing but like a heavenly message containing strength, hope, confidence, goodness, and power. It was then that the Lord burned the meaning of faith into my Mother's soul, and she *knew*. I had heard this story since I was young and I never once questioned my mom's experience but rather marveled in the happening she felt. My mom's experience comforted her through the anxieties of her life and continued to remain part of her affirmation of faith.

As a new wife, mother, business owner coping with those anxieties, I began to pray for such an obvious sign to affirm my faith. Any sign would do – a light, a vision, a burning bush – I didn't know how this miracle stuff worked so anything could count. I just wanted something to **see** so that I could **know.**

About six months following David's aneurysm I was at home reflecting on the experiences we had gone through. I walked through the many miracles we had witnessed; the silent whisper in the stinky truck; a messenger delivered to call for prayers; a life-saving surgeon hundreds of miles away. A light bulb went off and stopped me in my tracks. *Could it be? Had I been given a sign?!* It wasn't a divine light or burning bush but a series of small miracles that led me to a deeper knowing of God. Through the experience, I had developed an absolute trust that God is *for real*. A smile spread across my face as I thought, *Really, my husband had to go into a seizure, nearly die and suffer through brain surgery as an answer to my prayers?* I am sure that was not God's purpose for David's suffering, but it definitely got the point across!

Absolutely stunned at that realization, I began crying but not for sadness, yet out of fulfillment for a deeper understanding of God's presence in my life. I felt humbled for this gift. I then recognized the peace I had come to feel over the past few months about death and dying. Through David's experience I was forced to face my biggest fear, death, head on and conquer it. The fear of death no longer held onto me. I bowed my head in prayer and thanked Him for such an incredible awakening.

ACKNOWLEDGEMENTS

Thank you to Dr. Michelle Kelley (pictured right) and her office team. We have learned the actions of their team in those first moments of the rupture were instrumental in the success of David's full recovery. Thank you to Dr. Chicoine, all the nurses and staff at Barnes Jewish. Thank you to our families, church family and close friends that offered support, spent time at the hospital with David or me, and offered food, help and prayers during that time. Thank you for the specific gestures of love that helped us survive – sitting with David in the hospital, shipping me clothes and shoes to the hospital in St. Louis, making meals for our family, watching our dogs, and even getting my car to the airport. Thank you, Carol, for caring for and loving our children during that time. I know you gave them hugs and comfort when they needed comforting and didn't know what to think of what was going on. Thank you to our SeekingSitters office team for the support you gave David and me and the franchise system during David's time in St. Louis. Thank you to my mom, for your support and your hand to hold in the scary times of life. And thank you to those that helped me tell this story better than I could have on my own: Joanne Whitney, Katherine Haskell, and Forrest Cameron.

And mostly thank you to my husband – the rock in

my life – thank you for being strong for me when I was supposed to be the strong one for you. Thank you for always loving me and for your patience during my ever so often squirrel moments, like this book. I love you.

      A special thank you to CaringBridge. The support from family and friends poured in during David's time in the hospital. We wouldn't have been able to keep everyone updated without the help of the CaringBridge website and the messages we received kept us strong.

      By the time David was released from the hospital in St. Louis there were 3,200 views on the CaringBridge website from family, friends and friends of friends and over 500 messages and prayers were posted throughout his stay. Listed below are just a few of the messages and prayers that inspired us during our time and we would like to share them with you.

Wednesday, October 21, 2009

      Dear A,

      I am so sorry that this happened. I am also so glad that it ended as it did, here in St. Louis. You are in great hands with the team of doctors at Barnes. Please call me. I am ready to help in any way that I can. Honest, call anytime even middle of the night. I will keep the phone close by. Also make sure you get some rest too. I am sure you are not sleeping at all...Love you lots!

      Mary Kaiser

Wednesday, October 21, 2009

      To: David and family,

      We have been reading all the messages. One would think everything that could be said has already been said, but a few hundred more messages could not possibly explain how much you mean to so many people, especially to us. You are certainly in our prayers and on the prayer list at South Tulsa Baptist Church. We will send you a copy of our Wednesday night "table talk". You are now on a whole lot more prayer lists. Although Ann is fairly new to SeekingSitters, Floyd feels like he has known you and Adrienne for a long time because of everything Ann has told him about you. So many of Ann's clients have said so many great things about you and we are sure most of them are praying for your recovery. We would all like for it to be speedy, but God works in HIS time frame, so we pray for a complete recovery and will give HIM the glory when it is completed.

Ann Allen

Wednesday, October 21, 2009

David,

I am so amazed by you! You are doing so well! We have been worrying about you and praying for you! We hope you know that the covenanter's class and others from the church are here for you now and especially when you get back to Tulsa! Please let us know if there is a need we can help with and we'll do our best! I want the words "Church Family" to ring true! Hang in there both of you and we can't wait to see you again soon!

Lisa & Adam Marshall

Wednesday, October 21, 2009

David, Adrienne, and kiddos - I am stunned! But I thank God that David is doing well...we pray that he has a quick recovery and able to get out of that hospital room and back to T-Town! Sounds like he is in good hands. We will keep checking for updates.

Amy and James St. Peter

Wednesday, October 21, 2009

Adrienne and Family,

199

Jerry and I just got the email about David and we are sending our love and prayers to all of you. We're thankful that the surgery went well and that David is doing as well as could be expected. Keep the faith and know that a whole lot of prayers are being said and we hope David will have a quick recovery. God is never too tired to carry us through these trials and we're so thankful for his mercy.
Jerry & Liz Baker

Wednesday, October 21, 2009

We're glad to hear that David is doing well. You have our prayers and love and support. We're here for you if you need anything.

I'm glad you've been able to keep your sense of humor through all of this. Laughter heals! Did you hear the one about.... wait this is a public forum right???
John Schaffitzel

Wednesday, October 21, 2009

Go Super-David Go! We love you and are sending as much healing power your way as we can muster up!
XOXO
The Other Whitneys

Wednesday, October 21, 2009

David & Adrienne,

You're so loved and thought about often throughout these last few days. Praying for a speedy recovery and a handsome military cut! Can't wait to hear more progress of your good news. ;)
Lots of Love,
Megan Boyle

Wednesday, October 21, 2009

OH David and Big A.

You all take care and get lots of rest and we hope you are on the mend soon! You have many friends and loved ones here praying for you all and please

lean on us because you can! And you most certainly should...that's what friendship is all about. If you need us please don't hesitate to call! God speed to a full and quick recovery!
Alicia & Scott Champion

Wednesday, October 21, 2009

Hey David-

Just remember Psalms 142:3. "When your Spirit grows weak within you, it is the Lord who knows your way."

You guys are in our prayers.

Amy & John Laguna

Wednesday, October 21, 2009

My prayers and thoughts are with everyone in St. Louis.

Aaron Whitney

Wednesday, October 21, 2009

Hey there boss –

When you get done there will you come back please :) I'll make sure the coffee is fresh! Oh and can I have a raise?? Hee Hee! We miss ya!

Christina Oliver

Wednesday, October 21, 2009

David and Adrienne,

I could not believe when I heard the news but I am so glad the surgery is done and that they caught it in time. Please know both of you and the doctors and your entire family are in my thoughts and prayers. I have also put out prayer requests to everyone I know. May God bless you and watch over you during your recovery period. Get well and get back to Tulsa soon so you can call us again :)

Tanecia Kirkland

Wednesday, October 21, 2009

Kallweit Family,

My Prayers are with you! Let me know if there is

anything at all you need. All of the sitters are here for you! And don't worry!!! Christina can hold down fort just fine!

Brandy Boren

Thursday, October 22, 2009

You scared the crap out of us buddy! Glad to hear things are progressing. I don't usually pray about getting a chance to drink another cold one with somebody, but in your case I made an exception. Looking forward to following through with that request. Hope we see you back in the saddle again soon.

David White

Thursday, October 22, 2009

Dave and Adrienne,

Just wanted to let you know we're thinking of you and praying for the best. You hang in there Dave and get better as soon as you can. I was just thinking it's about time the four "Richards" got together again and partied so keep that in mind as you recover!! We'll get something worked out. I'll keep checking back and I want to hear good news each day. You'll make it. Just stay strong.

Jeff and Carol Maddox

Thursday, October 22, 2009

D & A,

You are in our prayers all throughout the day and 24/7. Your strength, courage, love and zest for life is so amazing and a testament to us all. We are really pulling for you... And feel like if anyone could beat this, it's you two as a team!!!! Keep up your positive attitude, awesome faith and keep your focus. Know that the prayer chain is strong in Houston. Thank you for this website and keeping us updated. Love to you both, D & A:)

Cousin Maralee, Mike and Anna

Thursday, October 22, 2009

Hey Kallweits.

So glad to hear the news that all is going as expected. Please know that you are being lifted up in prayer and we can't wait to surround you with love in person! What a testimony you will have! Let me know if there is anything I can do, especially for the kiddos, right now. Adrienne, take care of yourself too!

Blessings,

Jan Miller

Thursday, October 22, 2009

David & Adrienne

Been thinking about you non-stop. We missed you both last night as I had two extra passes for Corporate Night at Oktoberfest that I was going to surprise you with. It wasn't the same without you.

Your strength amazes me - please do not hesitate to call on me for help with anything.

You are both an inspiration and what an amazing story. I always knew you were incredible people - but this journey proves it. What a great testament to your marriage and relationship.

Give David our love. You are in our prayers constantly.

We love you

Diane, David and Jameson White

Thursday, October 22, 2009

David and Adrienne, my heart aches that you have had to undertake this journey; but my heart is also confident and proud to know that you two will prevail and turn this into a successful learning experience. I am happy to hear that you are receiving top notch care.

Please let me know if I can do anything for you now or in the future. You have many fine people thinking about you and your speedy and complete recovery.

Chin up! Call anytime!

Buck Cowen

Thursday, October 22, 2009

Adrienne and David,

Just got the link to this website. So relieved to finally get some more information. Ryan called me Tuesday morning and you have both been in our prayers ever since. I contacted JoAnna and Leigh and we just wanted to fly right up there to be with you Adrienne. I am so glad you have your family there and that everything is going so well.

Clay and I will continue to pray and we have your family on several prayer lists including my mom's up in OKC, so you are just getting prayers from all around.

Please let us know how we can help now or in the future. We are all ready to help in any way possible.

Much Love,

Clay, Lindley and Charlie Welch

Thursday, October 22, 2009

I hate to hear about what happen. If there is anything you guys need, be sure and try everyone else before you call me (Joking) Please keep me posted, and call me when you get back into town so I can swing by and see you guys (Be sure and put the kids up first)

Take Care,

David Hall

Sunday, October 25, 2009

Wow! They make you folks from Oklahoma sturdy! I am thrilled to hear, David, that you are doing so well in such a short time after surgery. God has blessed both you and Adrienne and will continue to be there for you through your journey. As will all of us who are blessed to be a part of your lives.

Kim Kane

Sunday, October 25, 2009

Hi Guys

So happy things are going so well. David is certainly amazing. I bet they put this one in the book as their best success story. The staff must be so fabulous at that hospital. I feel that God did have a hand in getting you to the right place at the right time. A BIG hug for both of you and can't wait for you to come home.

Kay Graham

Monday, October 26, 2009

David and Adrienne,

I have been thinking about your family since the message went out about David. Glad to hear that David is recovering and is going back to his witty self again. Your family is so strong and Adrienne, never forget that you have tons of people who love your family and will be there in whatever way you need. David....you get better and don't give those nurses too hard of a time!

Harmony DeRose

Tuesday, October 27, 2009

Adrienne, we love you all so much. I am so thankful for your strength, as you have given so much from within to David. David is so blessed to have so much love surrounding him from far and near. Our prayers continue every day, from dawns early light, to the time we tuck ourselves into bed.

David is a winner, and he will be another miracle the doctors will be talking about for a long, long time. Our love and prayers,

Love, Kippy & Raymond

Tuesday, October 27, 2009

Oh, Adrienne, how strong you are and he is right, it

is not his time. I wish I were closer to help with the kids but I do know that you have that covered with all the loving family and friends. We think of you every day and I know you will be busy while you are in Tulsa making the kids feel comfortable with the whole situation. They are resilient and will be ok. Do take care of yourself as I am sure you are the last person you are thinking of right now. We all love you and the family you have created with SeekingSitters. You have both truly changed lives. Hugs, love and prayers,

Cecilia Giamundo

Thursday, October 29, 2009

David,

Now when you get out of ICU does that mean we can sneak you a beer? Sounds like you're doing great so keep it up and take your time getting well as we are watching over things here in Tulsa. PS: Will they let you watch the OU - Nebraska game it might be too much stress. If you like I'll tell you the score after the game is over.

Love you and stay strong.

Ben Whitney

Saturday, October 31, 2009

This is AMAZING news! I can't believe how well he's doing. What a miracle. Kisses to all. Happy Halloween!

Katherine Haskell

Sunday, November 1, 2009

Happy Halloween Kallweit Family:

Yes, even on Halloween night YOU are in our prayers for a speedy recovery. We do not understand suffering, but it is a part of our life if we are to be followers of Jesus. His life was 1/4 joyful, 1/4 glorious, 1/4 luminous and 1/4 sorrowful. David, we can see the light of God shining through you during these tough times.

Jean Selman

Thursday, November 5, 2009

David, I am so glad to hear you will be getting out of ICU- that is a step in the right direction. Brett and I will continue to pray for a full and speedy recovery!! Try to follow the nurse's orders- they do know what they are doing most of the time. :) You and Adrienne are strong people!! Try to rest.

Carey Baker

Thursday, November 5, 2009

Hi David:

Hey was it ever great to hear from you and get some news. No one can keep you down - eh? I know the saying is true - "If God takes you to it God will see you through it" and did He ever. Wow what a wonderful power. As to our precious Adrienne - She is an angel sent from God. She has been so wonderful keeping us all up to date and we really appreciate it. Take care and God Bless all of you. Give your family a hug for us.

Deanna Bell

Saturday, November 7, 2009

That is such wonderful news that he is coming home. There is truly no place like home and he will heal so much better in comfortable surroundings. We are so proud of him and you and the strength you have shown throughout this ordeal. We are keeping you guys in our thoughts and prayers.

Tracy Kennedy

Saturday, November 7, 2009

Oh my goodness! What a fantastic gift to be home for the holidays. I doubt few Christmases and Thanksgiving will top this one! Let's give thanks and a lot of "ho ho ho's" for such a remarkable recovery this season.

207

David, you have the strength of many and the determination of a few. What a superb job you, Adrienne, and your family and friends have done to get you back home and leading a normal, happy productive life. Hang in there Adrienne. Seeing how you two are getting through this with high hopes and how you two are pulling together is an inspiration to everyone.

Pause for a moment before stepping inside your house when you come home. Take in those few seconds when you step inside and realize that your place in the world is still there for you, that it always has been, and just how much it needs you. You are one of the few that will really know what it means to "come home again".

Congratulations to you and your family. Life doesn't get any better than this!

Marilyn Boyce

Sunday, November 8, 2009

We are so so happy for you David and all your family. God is good! And miracles continue to happen.

Love and God Speed

Sharon and Forrest Cameron

Monday, November 9, 2009

Whoopee! Hallelujah! You're coming home! Our prayers for you have been answered! We thought Adrienne was just kidding when she said you had sneaked out of the hospital to get to a TV to see the OU-Nebraska game! Nebraska kicked OU's butt and YOU kicked that aneurysm's butt! (Does an aneurysm have a butt? The way your doctor described it, it sounded like that aneurysm had several butts and maybe three arms and legs!) Talk about a fighter and a winner! The big winner (for life) goes to DHK! How thankful we all are! Against all odds but for the saving grace of the Lord, you are with us! We love you, David! Can't wait to see you!

JoJo Whitney

Monday, November 9, 2009

David,   all   I   can   say   is...WOW...you   ARE awesome! You did it! I wish I could be there with you to share in this happy occasion and celebrate with all the people that love you so, so much...talk about truly **HAPPY** hours!

With the up-most sincerity, I want to congratulate you for being a true example of a survivor. You are testament to us all- courage, persistence, strength,   body,   mind   and   spirit. You   look   so   good   in   the   pictures! I am so happy for You, Adrienne and the Kids. I can only imagine the housewarming you all will experience...Definitely a milestone in the ABCDE lifetime. I hope that when you return home you will   continue   keeping   us   updated. WAY   TO   GO   DAVID!!!   YOU   DID   IT!!! With   so   much   love   and   excitement, Cousin Maralee

Monday, November 9, 2009

Hey David!

So glad you're on your way home. We're so thankful that all is well and that you'll soon be back to 100%. Guess the saying is right, "You can't keep a good man down." We'll see ya soon brother!

Ken & Merritt Graham

Monday, November 16, 2009

Hi David and Adrienne!

Thank you so much for emailing this link to me! I am so glad that everything went so well considering all that it took to get you to St. Louis. Glad to see that you're getting home and back to some normalcy in your lives! It was a great pleasure to accompany you in your flight. God is amazing! Lisa Leifheit (AeroCare Flight Transport)

Tuesday, November 17, 2009

What GLORIOUS news it is to hear that David is home and doing so well!! Yes, every day is a GIFT. And David is meant to be here for "such a time as this". God has tremendous plans in store for him and your family!!

Love U all so much,

Katie Ruley

Tuesday, November 17, 2009

I am sitting here crying at what good news you have just shared. The Lord is so evident in this healing! I want to tell everyone. We have been praying for you and are thrilled that the Lord is answering our prayers. I love it when He does that! Isn't it so funny that we all take our health for granted?! I do it every day. I recently spoke with someone who has been in a cast for several weeks and she was complaining about having to get everyone to help her do stuff. Isn't she blessed that she has people in her life with which to ask? David..I know that you are so thankful for Adrienne and your entire family that has been able to be there and be by your side.

It's been wonderful to watch everyone rally around you and pray for you. We will continue to pray for complete healing. We love you guys!

Shannon Wilburn

REFERENCES

If the reader would be interested in looking at the Barnes Jewish Hospital information, history and statistics related to neurosurgery, please go to:
http://www.barnesjewish.org/neurociences.

ABOUT THE AUTHOR

This book is about various events that have impacted my life and my hope is that in some way these stories will inspire you. I thank you for taking the time to read *Experiencing Love.* Please pass this story on to others as I feel we all have so much to learn from each other about how to move through hard times, reach out for support, and find answers. I continue to learn every day and look forward to the next adventure.

I can speak on this topic or other business related topics and would love to hear from you. Please contact me for speaking engagements or just to share your story at the following:

www.adriennekallweit.com
SeekingSitters Franchise System, Inc.
3144 S. Winston Avenue
Tulsa, OK 74135

9686392R0012

Made in the USA
Charleston, SC
03 October 2011